D1250735

MARCHAL E. LANDGREN

Robert Loftin Newman

1827–1912

PUBLISHED FOR
THE NATIONAL COLLECTION OF FINE ARTS
BY THE SMITHSONIAN INSTITUTION PRESS
CITY OF WASHINGTON 1974

OCTOBER 26, 1973–JANUARY 6, 1974 *National Collection of Fine Arts* *Smithsonian Institution, Washington, D.C.*

FEBRUARY 8–APRIL 28, 1974 *Tennessee Fine Arts Center, Cheekwood* *Nashville, Tennessee*

COVER: *Wood and Figures*, fig. 44, cat. no. 155.

FRONTISPIECE: Robert Loftin Newman.
Photograph by George C. Cox, New York, about 1890.
Cox Collection, Division of Graphic Arts,
Smithsonian Institution.

LIBRARY OF CONGRESS CATALOGING IN PUBLICATION DATA
Landgren, Marchal E.
Robert Loftin Newman (1827–1912).
Bibliography: p.
1. Newman, Robert Loftin, 1827–1912.
I. Smithsonian Institution. National Collection
of Fine Arts.
ND237.N48L36 759.13 73–15621

SMITHSONIAN INSTITUTION PRESS PUBLICATION NUMBER 4990
For sale by the Superintendent of Documents
United States Government Printing Office
Washington, D.C. 20402
Price: $5.45
Stock number: 4703-00023

To the Memory of the late Walter Sharp

Color is to a painting what style is to a work of literature. There are authors who think; there are painters who perceive . . . but in all times style and color have been precious and rare things.

DENIS DIDEROT

Contents

Acknowledgments

MARCHAL E. LANDGREN

I am greatly indebted to the many owners of paintings and drawings by Robert Loftin Newman, who over the years have permitted me to examine and record the works in their possession, and to the art dealers, especially the Vose Galleries of Boston, the Babcock Galleries, M. Knoedler & Company, Victor D. Spark, and the Graham Gallery, all of New York, who have given me access to their records on Newman. The early records of the Frank K. M. Rehn Gallery and those of the now-defunct Macbeth Gallery, both of New York, and the ledgers of the auctioneer Thomas E. Kirby were made available to me by the Archives of American Art.

In attempting to reconstruct the life of the artist from the little documentation that exists, I am especially grateful to Mrs. Walter Sharp of Brentwood, Tennessee, who turned over to me the papers on Newman collected by her late husband, who spent a number of years in the study of Newman, and to Mrs. Harold Allen Denis of Nashville, Tennessee, Newman's great-niece, who generously shared with both Mr. Sharp and me the results of her patient perusals of the Newman family records in Montgomery County, Tennessee. Dr. Thomas Brumbaugh of the Department of Fine Arts, Vanderbilt University, kindly sent me a copy before publication of his article "Letters of Robert Loftin Newman, a Tennessee Artist," which deals chiefly with Newman's correspondence with William W. Fergusson during the winter months of 1872–1873. The staffs of the Tennessee State Library and Archives, Nashville, the National Archives, Washington, D.C., the Frick Art Reference Library, New York, and the Long Island Historical Society, Brooklyn, New York, have been most cooperative and helpful.

During the early stages of research on Newman's life and works, invaluable assistance was given by Mrs. Alexander W. Drake, Mrs. Daniel Chester French, Mr. Samuel A. Chapin, and Mr. Robert Underwood Johnson, all of whom have passed from this life, but who during their late years willingly shared their reminiscences of the artist with me.

I owe the opportunity of preparing this monograph to Dr. Joshua C. Taylor, Director of the National Collection of Fine Arts, whose interest in Newman is part of his larger interest in the many diverse problems related to the study of the artist in America. I wish to thank him and the many members of his staff who assisted in the preparation of this monograph and the exhibition of Newman's work in connection with which it is published.

Introduction

JOSHUA C. TAYLOR
Director, National Collection of Fine Arts

Many years ago, while a student in a museum art school, I was very much taken with a tiny painting, probably one of the smallest in the museum collection, which seemed to consist of nothing more than a jagged spot of brilliant red punctuated with a vague dash of yellow, radiating mysteriously in an indeterminate sea of dense blue-green. It was in no sense an abstraction: the label explained that it was a representation of *Christ Lifting Peter from the Waves.* Yet what has remained indelibly in my mind all of these years is a memory of the strange radiance that seemed to belong to the colors themselves, but which I recognized at once as belonging also to my private world of feelings and reflection.

The works of Robert Loftin Newman—it was his painting that had caught my eye and became a part of my thinking—more often than not, I was to find, have this nagging strangeness. They make their impact quickly and simply, but remain hauntingly in the mind. Although there is no questioning the character of mood they evoke, the subject matter is often elusive. Each painting becomes, in its way, its own subject matter, with levels of meaning dependent on the speculative mind of the observer.

At first thought, Newman seems not to have sprung directly from any established American tradition; when he began to paint his small evocative paintings, most artists in America, if we can believe the critics of the time, were still directing their attention to the verities of nature and the niceties of optical truth. Imagination, always a word to conjure with, applied more often to subject matter than to form. The notion of art as evocation, however, evocation of emotion through the persuasion of the senses, was not long to be denied.

In 1846 Edgar Allan Poe, the difficult but compelling American author, wrote a modest but surprising essay called, "The Philosophy of Composition." Purporting to describe how he had composed *The Raven,* he proposed the thesis that a poet chooses each image and sequence of sounds in a deliberate effort to evoke a determined effect in the reader. That effect—and he realized how widely the word might be interpreted—was the aim of the poet's composition and, indeed, the meaning, the *raison d'être,* of the work of art. In fact, reading *The Raven,* it is true, produces an effect that cannot well be described without reference back to the fabric of the poem itself. It cannot be paraphrased. The effect and the composition are inseparable.

Although Poe's ideas on art may not have had a far-reaching impact in America at the time, they found a receptive ear in France. They were seized upon by Charles Baudelaire, who translated this particular essay in 1853, and were the source of inspiration to Stéphane Mallarmé as he formulated his own ideas of art in the 1860s. While the concept here suggested would be graced with the term Symbolist only later, it was already working its way through the arts in Europe by the late 1860s, to provide an antidote to what eventually would be condemned as a mindless viewing of nature.

At what point and just how Newman moved into this sphere of thought cannot be determined exactly, nor is it known how consciously he embraced the theoretical bases that seem to underlie so much of his work. Probably many painters of monumental canvases were more aware than Newman of a philosophical stance that would give special meaning to their paintings, but Newman's tiny images often say what their extensive allegories could not. Certainly it was in France, not America, that he discovered the pictorial means that would satisfy his artistic ends, and probably it was there also that he found the poetic environment in which his works take their being. He was drawn to the painters of Barbizon but also eventually shared his French colleagues' rediscovery of Delacroix, and their new interest in small, painterly canvases that carried the bravura of the eighteenth century to a whole new level of meaning. Yet Newman's paintings are quite distinct from those of his French contemporaries. Although at times passages recall the color of Delacroix, the richly painted figure studies of Diaz de la Peña, or the crepuscular fantasies of Adolphe Monticelli, there is a personal quality that does not quite fit into the French scene. A feeling of isolation often dominates even the most animated of compositions, cutting off Newman's sprightly figures from the world around. The haunting overtone of his paintings is not quite the same either—nor is it in precisely the same category—as those generated by the works of George Fuller, Ralph Blakelock, Albert Ryder, or other of the late nineteenth-century imaginative painters in America. Blown about in a shadowy world which seems to have no time nor boundaries, his staunch but unheroic figures, tiny though they may be, demand our participation and provoke our sympathy in a peculiarly characteristic way. The vitality of their being seems to radiate, even though their substance is no more palpable than the deftly colored shapes that bring them to mind. And it is in the mind they dwell, not in the observable world of the impressionist, nor even the prized world of previous art historical experience, which gave a special flavor to the works of some of Newman's contemporaries.

Robert Loftin Newman, then, was an individual in his approach to art, not the member of a school or a stylistic trend. He has often been noted as such. There has, in fact, been a degree of sentiment developed about his solitary position, as there has about the solitary positions of Blakelock, Ryder, and others of that generation. But the idea of the artist as a solitary—that is, as existing outside the larger social groups—was itself an aesthetic premise of the late nineteenth century, calling forth a distinctive kind of critical support. The following generation would intensify the association between the sentiment of loneliness and art. The artist was considered to be generally an exceptional person, but his exceptional qualities might be described as the mark of Olympian genius, as the sensibility of a *poète maudit,* or as the piquant manifestations of a genial Bohemian. Probably it was from an association with the second of these categories that Newman drew a part of his character. "This certain taint of sadness," Poe once wrote, "is inseparably connected with all the higher manifestations of true beauty." If Newman was indeed alone in his often melancholy pursuit, he was alone with a great many other solitary artists and doubtless took inspiration from the fact.

It is with the proliferation of styles and categories beginning in the 1870s that Newman's work belongs, a proliferation in which artists tended to group themselves by sentiment rather than by technique or subject matter. And a major sentiment was that pertaining to the artist himself, the artist as a builder of unique structures in experience, as a man who found meaningful pleasure where others saw only things. To be isolated was to belong to a particular world of art.

With a relaxation of some of our preconceptions about late nineteenth-century art in America, it may be that Newman, looked at afresh, will emerge not as a personal and historical misfit, but as an individual among individuals. As the group of cultural mavericks of the period grows larger, it is time to reassess the meaning of what we have considered to be nonconformity. Possibly our historical generalizations are at fault.

We are very grateful to Mr. Marchal Landgren, who has brought the knowledge gained from a long association with the works of Newman to the present study, for providing us with the first extensive catalog of Newman's work, and for his essay with its very personal interpretation of the place of Newman in modern art.

Robert Loftin Newman (1827-1912)

I THE LIFE OF THE ARTIST

Robert Loftin Newman is one of the most elusive figures in the history of American art. Only one exhibition of his work was held during his lifetime, and that took place in 1894, when he was almost seventy years of age. Only two of his paintings—one in 1849, the other in 1886—had been shown earlier in the annual exhibitions held in this country, which like the Paris Salons, were the artist's usual path to recognition. Nevertheless, his work entered most of the important art collections of his day, sometimes in astonishing numbers, so that it can be said that he held the equivocal position of recognition without recognition. Similarly, the position he held in relation to his peers is also equivocal. Born in the second half of the 1820s, he is of the generation of Sanford R. Gifford, James Francis Cropsey, William Morris Hunt, Eastman Johnson, George Inness, William P. Babcock, and Frederic E. Church. Excepting Hunt and Babcock, however, whom he had known as pupils of Thomas Couture and as friends of J. F. Millet's, he had little association with the artists of his own generation. It was the artists of the generation born around 1850, Albert Pinkham Ryder, William Merritt Chase, Wyatt Eaton, Francis Lathrop, and Daniel Chester French, who befriended and supported him. To them, he was "old Newman." He was neither of their generation nor of his own.

More exhibitions of his work have been held since his death in 1912 than were held during his lifetime, the first in 1924, and others in 1935, 1939, 1942, and 1961. Yet, even today, he remains an obscure, almost unknown figure, without public acceptance.

Newman was born at Richmond, Virginia, on November 10, 1827, the second and last child, and only son, of Robert L. and Sarah J. (Matthews) Newman. His sister, Eliza Jane, was born on August 26, 1823, also at Richmond. Newman's father died when he was a young child, and in 1832 his mother remarried, becoming the wife of Joseph Winston. In 1839, when Robert was eleven

Robert Loftin Newman.
Photographed by William P. Babcock,
Barbizon, 1882.

years old, the family moved to Clarksville, Tennessee, a college town and a prospering center of the tobacco industry near Nashville.

Little is known of Newman's early years. His sister, Eliza Jane, married John Lemmons at Clarksville in 1842. His stepfather, Joseph Winston, died in 1844. Newman was then left alone with his widowed mother.

It is said that he read much about art, and he himself wrote in 1872: "At college, I had eagerly devoured histories, biographies, essays, romances, poems, recounting the glory and splendor of Titian, Paul Veronese, Leonardo da Vinci, Raphael, Correggio, Guido, Rembrandt, Rubens, Holbein, Vandyck and their host of followers."[1] By the time he had reached his nineteenth year he had tried his hand at portrait painting, but feeling inadequate to the task he wrote to Asher B. Durand in New York asking to be taken on as a pupil, saying that he had "come to the determination of making a cast in another stream."[2]

At the time that Newman wrote to him on December 22, 1846, Durand was serving as president of the National Academy of Design, a position he held from 1845 to 1861, and was probably the best known of American artists. He had left behind a career as one of the foremost engravers in the country and was devoting himself to painting. Newman knew of Durand, as he wrote in his letter, by his "works and high reputation as a painter." His desire to "cast in another stream," he wrote, came as a result of "copying from prints," many of which were undoubtedly the work of Durand.

Nothing came of Newman's appeal to Durand, and there is no record that Durand ever replied to it. But today the letter is the only record of Newman's early interest in art. In it, he wrote:

Two years ago I took it in my head to be an—no, a painter of portraits, and longed for an insight into the "Divine Science." My good mother persuaded me 'twas all nonsense, but I could not withstand the temptation, so I bought brushes and paints with some money my kind mother gave me although she gave it with more reluctance than I ever saw from her before. Oh she is a kind good mother and I remember what she told me as I started to Louisville, "My son," says she, "you have chosen your own path. I hope it may be a smooth one." I choke almost when I think of this, but hope, a deceiving Mistress, bids me look forward and strike the harder.

Most of the letter reads like a dialogue with himself, as if it were an entry in his personal journal:

I painted two portraits of a lawyer in this place. He promised to pay me the sum of $10 for them. I called on him and asked

2. *Girl and Baby,* cat. no. 72.

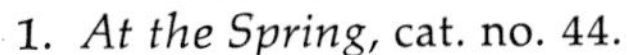

1. *At the Spring,* cat. no. 44.

him if he would have me send the portraits home. He said he thought I had better keep them as they might be of great benefit to me, or in other words act as "decoy Ducks" for others. I did the same thing for another knight of the bar and he served me likewise. I painted the portrait of a young physician and he begged it of me. I could not resist it so he took it home. It was my first attempt and I recollected the old adage, a bad beginning sometimes makes a good ending so comforting myself. *A young man engaged me to paint a portrait of his "Dark eyed lassie," I did so and worked on for two months trying to please him. He was never satisfied. His mind was continually changing, until the promised $10 disappeared from the horizon of hope. At last my mother seeing me so low spirited and down hearted told me to paint her picture. I tell you my dear Sir I was almost ashamed to* *face her after those disheartening attempts but, by dint of reading Cunningham's "Painters and Sculptors" (which is the only work which treats of artists I have ever read) I kept up my spirits and painted the picture. All that saw it knew it but although it soothed me to have this first praise, I could hardly bring myself to receive the ten dollars. I took and sent after more paints oils and brushes, having used up my entire stock of materials.*

Despite his failure to establish himself with Durand, Newman continued the copying of prints. Three years later, in 1849, the American Art-Union purchased his *Music on the Shop-Board,* an original subject that was exhibited in New York and, through the Art-Union's lottery, was awarded to a Mr. H. H. Muhlenburg of Reading, Pennsylvania.[3] Nothing is known of this early work today, but its title suggests a genre painting. Newman's stepfather was a tailor—his mother, a milliner—and the shop-board undoubtedly was the platform on which his stepfather had worked, used in this instance as a stage for musicians.

His First Trip Abroad

During the following year, 1850, Newman's yearning for pastures greener than those of "the glorious valley of the Mississippi," of which he was "heartily tired," according to his letter to Durand, and which was causing him to lose both his "time and temper," was temporarily appeased. He left Clarksville for his first sojourn abroad. The purchase of his painting by the American Art-Union had undoubtedly furthered both his ambition and his restlessness, and was probably the lever he used to pry himself away. His mother, as was her wont to do in later years, must have supplied the necessary funds.

According to Nestor Sanborn, a devoted friend of Newman's in later years, Newman was headed for study at Düsseldorf, a center that had begun to attract many Americans.[4] Emanuel Leutze had gone there in 1841 and his paintings were well known throughout America by engravings distributed by the American Art-Union and by reproductions published in contemporary journals. In Paris, however, Newman encountered William Morris Hunt (1824–1879) of Boston, who had found the academic training at Düsseldorf so rigid and stifling that he decided to give up painting for sculpture and had gone to Paris to study under James Pradier. Upon seeing Thomas Couture's painting *The Falconer* in a dealer's window, Hunt decided that if such work was painting, then he wished to be a painter. He sought out Couture and became one of his first American pupils.[5] When Newman arrived in Paris in 1850, Hunt

3. *Madonna and Child*, cat. no. 29.

was still with Couture and was to stay with him for two more years. Under Hunt's influence, Newman entered Couture's studio for a period of about five months. From the glorious valley of the Mississippi, Newman found himself, at the age of twenty-two, in the greenest valley of the art world.

The July monarchy had been overthrown, but Louis Napoleon had not yet declared himself emperor and a republican spirit still pervaded Paris. Enlightened criticism had begun to center on the work of Gustave Courbet, whose *Funeral at Ornans*, now in the Louvre, was shown at the Salon that year, and to a lesser degree, on the work of Jean François Millet, who had recently settled at Barbizon. Debate over the relative importance of color and line to the art of painting—and the one was seen to preclude the other—which could be traced back to the quarrel between the *Rubenistes* and the *Poussinistes* of the seventeenth century, now centered on the work of Delacroix and Ingres. Baudelaire had not yet published his eulogy of Delacroix, but had written substantially on him. Théophile Thoré, who defended Courbet, gave high praise to Delacroix in his "Salon of 1847" and, through his appreciation of color and of landscape painting, was paving the way for the advent of the Impressionists. Manet, eighteen years of age, had also just entered Couture's studio; Pissarro, twenty years old, was still living in his native St. Thomas in the Virgin Islands; Cézanne, eleven years old, was at Aix; and Monet, ten years old, at Le Havre.

In many ways, the situation in Paris in 1850 parallels the situation in America today. After the French Revolution, Paris became the creative center of the art world, much as New York did after the second World War. With wealth and power changing hands from generation to generation, then as now, the artist was placed in contention with successive waves of patronage, each emphasizing different aspects of his work. In 1850 and until shortly thereafter, the artist was content to let others speak for him. But he was soon forced to speak in his own behalf. Courbet led the way with his Pavilion du Réalisme at the world's fair of 1855, Manet joined with him in a similar venture at the world's fair of 1867, and their efforts culminated in the eight exhibitions organized by the Impressionists in their own behalf from 1874 to 1886. In America today, similar waves of patronage have carried on their crests the work of the abstract expressionists, the pop artists, the color-field painters, the lyrical abstractionists, and the neorealists, and the artist has been willing to let others speak for him.

Newman, "a tyro in art" as he described himself, entered the complex art world of Paris as an innocent. Transplanted from central Tennessee, his image of the world of art, gained vicariously from his reading, could not have included any sense of the reality of the professional life of the artist as it flourished in a world capital. Rivalries among advocates of one school of painting over another, of one master over another, to say nothing of the vicissitudes of patronage, although they must have been subjected to common talk among the students in Couture's studio, were beyond his experience, and he was not in Paris long enough to assimilate them.

4. *Mother and Child,* 1902, cat. no. 108.

The Influence of Couture

In many ways, Couture was the ideal teacher for Newman, and it was Newman's good fortune to have been directed to him by Hunt. In 1847, Couture had had an overwhelming success at the Salon with his *Romans of the Decadence,* a large work measuring fifteen by twenty-five feet, and had opened a studio to accommodate the many students that were coming to him from all over the world. The *Romans* received much critical attention, especially for its vibrant color, but the quality of the work that attracted students to Couture was undoubtedly, as described by the perceptive Thoré, "the marvel of this execution, aside from skill in drawing and beauty of color, is a deliberate brushstroke, free, unlabored, light, and yet very vigorous."[6] As Hunt had found Couture's teaching an antidote to the rigid training at Düsseldorf, other students found it the antidote to academic training in general.

The various components of Couture's way of painting were nothing new and can be traced to his training under Baron Gros and Paul Delaroche, as well as to certain notions then prevalent, such as the use of complementary colors and of the optical mixture of colors. What was significant was Couture's adaptation of these components to a method of painting that was not only eminently suited to his own facility in both drawing and painting, but was also easily communicated to his students.[7]

"Beauty of outline, beauty of masses, as beauty of color," he wrote in 1867, "require an incessant sacrifice of detail." His "method," as he called it, was directed to achieve this trinity, and fundamental to it were an observant eye and a well-trained hand. He advised his students, "Draw morning and evening to exercise your eyes, and to secure a good hand," and requested that they carry with them always a tablet on which "to sketch the beautiful things which you see, startling effects, natural positions" and to "use materials gained by your own observations."

A facility in drawing was essential to his method, which, stated simply, began with the drawing of the subject in charcoal on the canvas. The drawing was then outlined and the shadows were massed with a long-handled sable brush, dipped in a "sauce" of strong boiled oil and essence of turpentine, half and half, and then in a bistre tint, made of a mixture of bitumen and brown-red, or of cobalt and brown-red, "a kind of sepia tint." After this had dried overnight, he used the same preparations to set the light tones. When the latter had dried to a sticky state, he set his palette and painted in the lights, applying the pigment thick where the lights were the most intense and thin for the secondary lights. In mixing two or more colors on his brush, he advocated that they not be mixed thoroughly so that each color would preserve its integrity, thus achieving something of the optical mixture of colors so dominant later in the work of the Impressionists. Couture did not advise the mixing of more than three colors on the brush and preferred to use color pure, but if more than two or three colors were needed, he advised their rapid application in thin glazes. The method, with its carefully controlled scumbles and rapidly applied glazes, was intended to preserve the freshness of the sketch, the original conception, in the finished work. Its success in doing so was relative to the facility of the artist.

Newman studied with Couture for only a few months, and so far as is known, he received no other formal training. It must be assumed that he had acquired a certain skill in drawing before entering Couture's studio; otherwise, he could not, in such short a time, have comprehended a way of painting so dependent upon a correspondence of hand and eye. Moreover, Couture's method, which permitted much freedom in interpretation, must have been sympathetic to the expression of Newman's own feelings. Variations of it can be detected throughout the body of his known works. Düsseldorf would have stifled him, as it had threatened to stifle William Morris Hunt.

A comparison of Couture's *Fugitive* in the Brooklyn Museum (fig. 5) with Newman's *Prodigal Son* (fig. 6) shows how well Newman understood the massing of shadows and the application of the primary and secondary lights, as advocated by Couture. If the *Fugitive* reveals a bravura unknown to Newman, and the *Prodigal Son* a compassion unknown to Couture, such are the differences in the two men.

Couture was something of a braggart, and he placed his skills second to none. He took an independent stand in the critical quarrels of the day. Supporting neither Ingres nor Delacroix, he considered those who argued over color versus line ignorant, saying, "they do not know that all is in all." Of Delacroix, he said "what he does is incomplete, because he tries to give form to the darkness of his mind." As to the so-called Realists, he caricatured them in a painting called *The Realist* in which he portrays the artist, drawing board in hand, seated on a fragment of classical sculpture —an antique head—before his model, the head of a pig. In fact, he tried to belittle the work of his colleagues. John La Farge, who studied with him briefly in 1856, found himself annoyed by Couture's "constant running down of other artists greater than himself."[8] Nevertheless, Couture was a friendly man, who took an almost patriarchal interest in his students. Manet stayed with him for six years and afterward, often returned for criticism of his work.

To the neophyte Newman, untouched by the vagaries of the art world, Couture's independent stand, together with his insistence on skillful, vigorous brushwork, was an emphasis on the means of expression rather than on what was to be expressed. "Beauty of outline," "beauty of masses," and "beauty of color" became ends in themselves. Although Couture was persistently plagued by the need to impose rather commonplace anecdotal meaning on his work, the need usually got in his way. His most significant works are those based on direct observation. His criticism of Delacroix was based on Delacroix's choice of subjects, not on his methods. Similarly, he criticised Millet for his sentimental attachment to the

5. Thomas Couture. *The Fugitive.* The Brooklyn Museum.

peasant. If Millet had simply painted the peasant, instead of making him the subject of his sermons, Couture would no doubt have accepted his work. In a way, he criticised others for a weakness in himself. The farsighted Thoré, in his discussion of Couture's *Romans of the Decadence*, recognized that weakness when he wrote that the success of the *Romans* was an unhappy moment for Couture. Since it was a commonplace of the day to compare contemporary civilization with the downfall of Rome, Thoré noted that "the picture is destined to please everyone," adding that "unanimity is not as good as discussion."[9] In other words, a popular theme, presented with a certain flair and lively color, tended to obscure the painting's real qualities.

The Impact of the Louvre

Newman's other teacher during his short stay in Paris was the Louvre. There, he had his first encounter with the masterpieces of his chosen profession. His first reaction, as he wrote of it twenty-two years after the event, "was one of disappointment." His imagi-

6. *The Prodigal Son*, cat. no. 38.

7. Titian. *The Entombment*, ca. 1525, The Louvre, Paris.

nation, "heightened and inflamed" by reading the lives of the great masters, had "wrought visions which nothing short of the magic hues of an apparition would have appeased." With relief, he "turned from them to some of the meretricious and flashy works of the modern French school; works gorgeous in the colors of the toy book." He compared his disappointment with the experience of Joshua Reynolds, "who in his discourses remarks his chagrin on first inspecting the collection of the Vatican."[10]

"Study in the Life school and calm careful observation and comparison," Newman wrote, "dispelled these dreaming visions, the scales fell from the eyes and by diligent investigation a healthy taste for works of merit formed; feelings of disappointment wore off and humble admiration led me to approach them with awe and respect, a genuine tribute due their wonderful qualities." "Occasionally," he added, "I wandered off after strange gods, precedents sufficiently numerous existed to console me for those lapses from the true faith; at last spellbound I stood gazing on what seemed the unattainable!" He compared his experience with

The desire of the moth for the star
Of the night for the morrow,
The devotion to something afar
From the sphere of our sorrow.[11]

He questioned whether "duplicate Titians, Homers, Shakespeares,

8. *The Entombment,* cat. no. 13.

Jobs, Michael Angelos, Phidias's [were] necessary to the comfort and well-being of the human race." In a rather biting reference to the popular culture of his time, he asked whether Martin Farquhar Tupper had "toppled the preacher from the Throne of Wisdom."[12] He also questioned whether the methods of the great men of the past were communicable to the artists of the present day. "Yet," he added, "the solemn tones of the Entombment, deep, rich, glowing as jewels, rubies, garnets, sapphires, emeralds, amethysts, all were there in the entrancing hues of twilight, gorgeous in gloom . . . does any one who has studied the Entombment [fig. 7] forget the blue mantle and sorrowing looks of Mary, the robe of amethyst of Martha, the stooping man in dark lustrous green, the crimson splendor and solemn purple robes of the figure, holding the corpse-like body of the dead Christ, the woeful stillness in the air, the clouds lighted with bars of gold, and the blue sky deep as the immensity of space, the brown trees that seem to sigh and rustle in the evening breeze, the sombre earth humbly bearing upon its bosom the dead God."

"Titziano Vecelli del Cadore," he continued, "dipped his pencils in tones of splendor, visible to himself alone; he saw, where others were blind . . . his extraordinary power as a draughtsman is lost sight of in this sorcery of color."

Newman painted a small version of the *Entombment* (fig. 8).

One-tenth the size of the Titian, it was probably painted from memory. It includes an additional figure, six instead of five, and the position of the dead Christ is reversed, so that Joseph of Arimathea is at the feet of Christ, not at the head as in the painting by Titian. The little canvas is a most dramatic one, in which Newman interprets both the rhythm of the composition and the jewellike hues of the original, "all there in the entrancing hues of twilight." In his *Christ and the Apostles* (fig. 9), a major work, the twilight setting of the Titian reappears.

Other Titians in the *Salon Carré* of the Louvre that attracted Newman were the *Man with a Glove,* "hanging high up to the right," and the portrait of Francis I, "gorgeous in crimson sleeves, and cap and feather." He called Veronese's *Wedding Feast at Cana* "a Venetian banquet truly," and compared Leonardo's *Mona Lisa,* whose "intense black eyes have marvellous sweetness and depth," to the description of Diana given by Heinrich Heine in his *Reisebilder* as she is seen by the weary traveler in his dream, passing through the gorge of Roncesvalles. Newman was obviously compelled by the mountainous landscape against which Leonardo had placed his sitter. Newman also commented on the works of Giorgione, Correggio, Van Dyck, and Rembrandt. But it was the example of Titian that stayed with him. Those who knew him in his late years have recorded that he considered Titian the great master and that he gave Delacroix first place among the moderns.

Newman's Second Journey to Paris

Newman returned to Clarksville after his sojourn in Paris. As far as is known, he stayed there until 1854, when he again ventured abroad. To finance this second trip, his mother had signed notes amounting to almost $3,600, in return for which Newman, two years later, relinquished his interest in his stepfather's estate.[13]

At Paris, Newman renewed his friendship with William Morris Hunt, who in 1852 had given up his studies with Couture and had come under the influence of Millet at Barbizon. Hunt introduced Newman to Millet and to William P. Babcock, a fellow Bostonian, who in 1847 had also studied with Couture. Babcock, one of the first American artists to befriend Millet, had settled at Barbizon and was to spend most of his life there.

It was undoubtedly Hunt who also introduced Newman to another Bostonian, Nathaniel Greene. Greene, thirty years Newman's senior, had retired as postmaster of Boston in 1849 and was living abroad. He had also had a long career as a journalist and editor; in 1821, he founded the Boston *Statesman,* which became the leading Democratic paper in Massachusetts. In addition, Greene was a

9. *Christ and the Apostles,* cat. no. 5.

linguist with many translations to his credit, including Luigi Sforzosi's *Compendious History of Italy* (1836) and *Tales from the German, Italian and French* (1843). While in retirement and traveling in Europe, he wrote many poems that were published in Boston newspapers under the pseudonym Boscawen, the name of his birthplace in New Hampshire.

Greene and Newman shared an apartment on the fashionable Chausée d'Antin, where they lived more than well. "They kept a cook, had a well-stocked cellar and larder."[14] With the money Newman's mother had borrowed to finance his stay in Paris, Newman "indulged his taste for glass, armor, prints and paintings to the full, enjoying them with gusto." There is no inventory of his purchases. He reportedly purchased a Millet, *The Winnower;* and it is known that he owned a canvas by Manet's friend, Charles Monginot, who was probably Newman's fellow student at Couture's in 1850; and a canvas by Hunt.

Of the moneys raised to finance Newman's trip, $1,500 was borrowed from A. B. Barrett, a Kentucky tobacco planter, who happened to be in Paris at the time Newman was living with Greene. Barrett must have felt that his money was being squandered; no other explanation suffices. Obtaining the key to Newman's apartment held by the banker Munroe Leavitt Hunt, he confiscated, without warrant, the paintings, including the Millet, and other objects that Newman had purchased. Some years later, these objects were recovered by Newman from Barrett's son-in-law in New York, but the Millet was not among them. Quincy Shaw of Boston reported to Newman that he had seen it in other hands in Paris.

Newman made two trips to Barbizon. He went first with William Morris Hunt to visit Millet, and later with William Babcock. He reputedly spent a few months in the village.

There is no indication that Newman continued his studies or that he even did any work during his second stay in Paris. Nor is there any indication of the influence of Barbizon on his work at that time. What he did develop was a taste for the good things of life.

His Return to Clarksville

Newman returned to Clarksville and lived there, with his mother, until he was conscripted into the Confederate army in 1864.

Clarksville, situated on a penninsula at the confluence of the Cumberland River and the Red River, lies in a tobacco-growing district. Trade in tobacco had made it a prosperous town; it was particularly noted for its dark-fired tobacco, which was shipped by flatboat to New Orleans then to European markets. The city is built on seven hills, and in Newman's day, its tree-lined streets and riverbanks were the sites of many attractive homes.

The Newman-Winston residence, a modest story-and-a-half structure with dormer windows, was near the Masonic University of Tennessee, which in 1855 became Stewart College, named for its president, William M. Stewart. The college was housed in what has become known as the Old Castle Building, which, in turn, became the home of the Southwestern Presbyterian University in 1879 and of the Austin Peay Normal School in 1927. Newman's home was demolished in 1969.

There can be little doubt that Clarksville was an attractive town in which to live. Pleasantly situated and prosperous, it had much to offer in the ordinary pursuits of life. But there is also no doubt that it offered little to one of Newman's temperament. His stay there between 1854 and 1864 was more a matter of circumstance than of choice.

On November 12, 1858, he placed the following notice in the *Tobacco-Leaf Chronicle* and the *Jeffersonian*, the local newspapers:

Robert Newman will give instruction in Drawing during the winter to class of Ladies and Gentlemen. No pupils taken but those somewhat advanced in the art.

I will open a Studio at my residence, near the College, next Spring, and will devote a portion of time to painting whole length portraits.

If the Faculty of the College, and the committees of the several Male Schools of the city, will establish Drawing classes in their respective institutions, and place them under my government, I will instruct the classes free of charge as long as my health and time will permit of it. Having studied in the best schools of Europe I am well acquainted with the systems in favor there.

By teaching privately and by accepting commissions for full-length portraits, Newman sought to support himself. The offer to give instruction free of charge at the college and at the "several Male Schools" was, without doubt, an effort not only to show the skill he had acquired "in the best schools of Europe" but also to create a community of interest in the fine arts that Clarksville did not offer. The potential for such a community was certainly to be found among the students who had come to Clarksville for their education.

It is not known whether his offer was ever accepted. Two full-length portraits of the period, however, attributed to "Mr. Newman of Clarksville" are known. They are portraits of *Adelia Boisseau Warfield and Daughter Huldah Belle Warfield* and of her husband and son *William Wallace Warfield and Son* (figs. 10 and 11). They have passed down in the family to Leslie Cheek, Jr., of Richmond, Virginia—Huldah Belle Warfield was his maternal grandmother—and they are the only known works attributed to Newman from that period. Large works—each canvas is just over seven feet in height—they suggest little of Newman's later development, but then, Newman did not pursue a career in portraiture. The portraits once graced the double drawing room (designed to accommodate them) at Cheekwood, now the home of the Tennessee Fine Arts Center, Nashville.

Service with the Confederate Army

Newman was still at Clarksville when the Civil War broke out. He was "elected a lieutenant of artillery" and claimed to have "enlisted and swore into service about fifteen men," but a "disagreement occurring with the Commanding Officer" upon what he considered "a dishonorable enlistment of men," he resigned.[15]

He was, however, conscripted into service in the Confederate army and by early April 1864 was in Richmond, Virginia. From Richmond, he wrote two letters to Jefferson Davis, dated April 9, 1864, and April 11, 1864. In the first, he requested a position as aide-de-camp to a general's staff "to see the Campaign of 1864 to feel the shock of battle intellectually and physically" so that he might paint it, and he claimed to be physically unfit "to do duty

10. *Portrait of Adelia Boisseau Warfield and Daughter Huldah Belle Warfield*, ca. 1857, cat. no. 126.

in either Infantry, Cavalry, or Artillery." In the second, "wishing to be relieved from the odium and depression of the Conscription," he asked for a commission, even of the lowest grade, stating that he wished to continue his art. The letters were forwarded by Jefferson Davis to the secretary of war, James A. Seddon, to whom Newman also wrote, enclosing a certificate from Dr. James A. Conway of Richmond, dated April 12, 1864, which stated that Newman suffered "from an extraordinary varicose state of the veins" and was "utterly and permanently incapacitated for military duty."

11. *Portrait of William Wallace Warfield and Son,* ca. 1857, cat. no. 127.

Newman's letter to Seddon is dated April 18, 1864, but was probably written on April 28, the day that his letters to Jefferson Davis were forwarded to Seddon. In it Newman asked for either "an honorable position in the Army as an officer" or a discharge. His reason was that he wished to "go on with a large picture of the 'Rout at Manassas' fifteen by thirty five feet," which he claimed to have "in hand." To support his request, he cited the example of the French government "which during the War of the Crimea sent M. M. Horace Vernet and [Adolphe] Yvon to the scene of action to make studies, in the Italian Campaign M. Meis-

12. *Mother and Two Children,* cat. no. 116.

sonnier and Baume [Joseph Beaume?]." Furthermore, he noted that "the Honorable Secy has exempted from the conscription several historians Mssrs Pollard, Harrison, McMahon, etc." and proposed "to trace as brilliant a page" with his brush "as those gentlemen with their pens." His request was denied. "I can not find," was the reply of the secretary, "in the love or study of Art exemption from the duty imposed in Classic Antiquity as under Modern Civilization to all men save witnesses to God of defending their country against the invader."

Newman was enrolled on May 2, 1864, as a conscript at Camp Lee, Virginia. He was assigned on June 2 to the 15th Virginia Regiment, known as Corse's Brigade, Pickett's Division, at Richmond, but for some months was detailed to the naval ordnance works. On August 5, he requested employment as a draftsman in the engineer service. Captain John Mercer Brooke, who designed the ordnance and armor of the *Merrimac,* certified that he knew Mr. Newman, "whose profession is that of an artist." Although the records indicate that such employment was refused Newman at the time, it is probable that he gained it at a later date. Nestor Sanborn, the friend of Newman's late years, claims that Newman was "transferred to the Topographical Department."[16] In any event, the muster rolls show that he was in the division hospital at Chester Station during November and December and that on January 17, 1865, he was detailed to the Army of Northern Virginia under General Lee.

13. *The Finding of Moses,* 1899, cat. no. 14.

After the fall of Richmond, Newman, a conscript for the duration of the war, was released from service (April 18, 1865) and gave his destination as New York.

The Postwar Years

Nestor Sanborn's notes on Newman state that after leaving the service, Newman, on his way to New York, stopped at Baltimore, where he was employed for about a year "in a sign painter's loft, working at political banners."[17] The Montgomery County records, however, show that he was back in Clarksville on August 15, 1865. On that day, he and his mother sold a lot that they owned jointly to his sister's eldest daughter.[18] Whether he went directly to Clarksville from Richmond or whether he stopped at Baltimore on the way is not known. He probably left for New York after a brief stay at Clarksville.

During the winter of 1872–1873, Newman was at Nashville. He had taken a studio at 45½ Union Street, next door to the studio of George Dury (1817–1894), a portrait painter, who, with his brother-in-law Augustin Gattinger, a well-known botanist, had emigrated from Munich to Tennessee in 1849. With Dury, Newman attempted to establish an Academy of Fine Arts at Nashville. Together they tried to enlist the support of the community

14. *The Letter*, cat. no. 95.

and invited "all the Artists and Amateurs in town with Govr Brown and what Confederates that can be got together, the solid men of Nashville and the literary people, members of the press and some ladies" to a meeting on December 12 "for the purpose of consulting together and establishing an Academy of Fine Arts."[19] Nothing seems to have come of their venture.

Earlier in the year, on September 25, Newman had advertised that he would open a school in his studio,[20] and in November he wrote to a friend that he was teaching "a small class in one of the Public Schools."[21] Once again, as at Clarksville before the war, Newman was attempting to create a community favorable to the arts. The invitation to the meeting of December 12 stated that it was being held "for the purpose of conferring and consulting together as to the best means of advancing the cause of Art in our midst, and for the placing before the public examples in Casts from the finest works of the Greek Sculptures in Rome, Florence, Paris and London, and for obtaining such examples, good copies or originals, if practicable, of the master-pieces of the Italian, Spanish,

Flemish, French and English Schools, together with such other works as may be subservient to the cause of Art."[22]

Again Newman attempted to support himself by painting portraits; the Nashville city directory of 1873 lists him as a portrait painter. The death of his mother at about this time severed his close ties to central Tennessee.[23] New York was to become his second home.

The Move to New York

New York in the 1870s witnessed a major mutation in the professional life of the artist in America, perhaps the first major mutation in the series that has affected the course of the history of art in America.[24]

A new generation of artists, those born around 1850, entered into the artistic life of the city and reformed the means of both educating the artist and presenting his work to the public. Their reforms also set new standards of art criticism. The artists came fresh from their studies, principally from Paris and Munich. Among them were the sculptor Augustus Saint-Gaudens (1848–1907), the painters Wyatt Eaton (1849–1896), Will H. Low (1853–1932), and Julian Alden Weir (1852–1919), and the architect Stanford White (1853–1906), all from Paris; the painter William

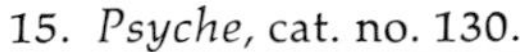

15. *Psyche,* cat. no. 130.

Merritt Chase (1849–1916), from Munich; and the painter and decorator Francis Lathrop (1849–1909), from London. They were joined by certain of their older contemporaries, notably by John La Farge (1835–1910) and Walter Shirlaw (1838–1909). What these men accomplished in New York by speaking out in their own defense against the policies of the National Academy parallels what was accomplished by Courbet and the Impressionists in Paris when they defied the policies of the Salon.

The critics, who took up their cause and changed the course of art criticism, included William Crary Brownell (1851–1928), who was on the staff of the *Nation* from 1879 to 1881; Charles de Kay (1848–1935), who became literary and art editor of the *New York Times* in 1877; and Clarence Cook (1828–1900), who began contributing to *Scribner's Monthly* and rejoined the staff of the *New York Tribune* as art critic in 1875.

A focal point of their activities was a house on East Fifteenth Street, set far back from the building line on the north side of the street, just east of Union Square. This was the house to which Richard Watson Gilder, then managing editor of *Scribner's Monthly,* had taken his bride Helena de Kay, a painter and the sister of Charles de Kay, after their marriage in 1874. As Will Low expressed it, the artists returning from Europe found "in the little house on 15th Street an oasis in the first few years of our return to our desert home, as it appeared to us in comparison to the flowery regions of art whence we came."[25]

The first attempt at change that took place at the house on Fifteenth Street was a meeting of artists directed toward holding a sort of *salon de refusés,* as a result of the National Academy's spring exhibition of 1875. Francis Lathrop was appointed a committee of one under John La Farge to organize the exhibition. The exhibition was held in the galleries of Cottier & Company, which had recently opened at 144 Fifth Avenue. Among the artists represented were William Morris Hunt, John La Farge, Francis Lathrop, Maria Oakey, Abbott H. Thayer, Helena de Kay, and Albert Pinkham Ryder. *Scribner's Monthly,* in a review probably written by Clarence Cook, reported that the exhibition was "made up in such a way as to represent only a certain style, or several kindred styles, of painting (especially those with which the Academy has little sympathy); and the circumstances suggest that it would be interesting to have frequent exhibitions on some such plan, in order to keep fully before our eyes what is going on in different directions among the artists."[26] Another critic claimed that "it represents one of the most important art movements of the day."[27]

Later that same year, 1875, the Art Students League of New York was founded by students dissatisfied with the instruction they were receiving at the National Academy. The League, a collection of private studios under one administration and one roof, with no

16. *The Wandering Mind,* cat. no. 152.

prescribed curriculum, and under the government of the students, became the most influential art school in America. Helena de Kay was an active member of the League, and Walter Shirlaw, William Merritt Chase, Augustus Saint-Gaudens, and Julian Alden Weir were among the artists who served as instructors during its early years.

In 1877, again in dissatisfaction with the policies of the National Academy, another meeting of artists was held in the Gilder home. The outcome was the establishment of the Society of American Artists for the purpose of holding annual exhibitions in competition with those of the Academy. Present at that meeting were Walter Shirlaw, who became the first president of the Society; Augustus Saint-Gaudens, who became vice-president; Wyatt Eaton, who became secretary; and Helena de Kay. Clarence Cook, who championed the cause of the Society in the pages of the *New York Tribune*, sat in on the meeting, as did Julian Alden Weir, who became one of its original members.

It was into this state of affairs, in which a new generation of artists was speaking for itself in opposition to the control of the art profession by an older generation, that Newman entered when he took up residence in New York. It was described as "chaotic" by Clarence Cook, who found

but a faint degree of cohesion and sympathy among those [artists] who remain at home. One is characterized as painting in the French style, another as painting in the English style, and still others as adherents and imitators of certain strong individualities among themselves.[28]

By 1880, however, William C. Brownell noted "the coincidence between the appearance [of the new painters] and the beginning of a new order, the Renaissance, so to speak of 1877."[29]

In New York, Newman soon came into communication with this younger generation of painters. It is not known who introduced him to their circle, but the fine hand of his old friend William Morris Hunt, who had introduced him to Couture in 1850 and to Millet in 1854, undoubtedly guided him. Without an independent income, Newman needed work to support himself and found employment with Francis Lathrop, working on designs for stained glass. Hunt, La Farge, and Lathrop were all friends. La Farge had studied with both Couture and Hunt, and he was an intimate of the Gilders. With Lathrop, he guided the exhibition at Cottier's in 1875, which was prompted by the meeting of artists at the Gilder home, and Hunt was the only member of Newman's generation included in that exhibition. It was undoubtedly through Hunt that Newman met Lathrop, who not only offered Newman employment, but was among the first to buy his paintings; he is known to have owned at least nine Newmans, including two versions of the *Christ and the Apostles* (fig. 9) and the *Prodigal Son* (fig. 6). Moreover, the editors who served with Richard Watson Gilder on *Scribner's Monthly* became Newman's first patrons.

Lathrop, whose family had taken him to Germany to live when he was still a youth, returned to this country and settled in New York in 1873, in his twenty-fourth year. He began his study of

17. *Mother and Child,* cat. no. 111.

art at the Royal Academy, Dresden, when very young, and on the advice of James McNeill Whistler continued his studies in London, where he was received into the most advanced art circles. He studied with Ford Maddox Brown, whose connections with the Nazarenes in Italy had importance for the Pre-Raphaelite Brotherhood and with Edward Coley Burne-Jones, who with Daniel Gabriel Rossetti and William Morris represented the so-called second wave of Pre-Raphaelitism. Before returning to America, he worked for William Morris and Company in the design of stained glass. Stimulated by the example of Morris, he set out on a career in the decorative arts, which was to include both mural decoration[30] and stained glass. He first came to general attention in 1876 as the principal assistant to John La Farge in the decoration of Henry Hobson Richardson's Trinity Church in Copley Square, Boston. With La Farge and Hunt—who, also in the 1870s, did the murals for the State Capitol at Albany, New York, of which Richardson was one of the architects—Lathrop stands at the beginning of the decorative arts movement in America, which was responsible for many murals and stained-glass windows of religious themes in the decoration of churches.

Newman worked for Lathrop a short while, when, as Nestor Sanborn put it, he found the work "too close . . . for his restless spirit and like a knight-errant he cut loose from convention and started 'paintin' on his own account."[31] His friendship with Lathrop, however, continued over the years, and its influence on him was great. It not only introduced the religious subject to Newman's work, but added to certain of his religious themes something of the Pre-Raphaelites' attention to detail in drawing, particularly noticeable in the *Holy Family* (fig. 18) and the *Madonna and Child* of 1897 (fig. 19), in which the features of the Mother and Child are delineated with a care generally absent from Newman's work. Moreover, it brought Newman closer to the young generation of artists at the moment they began to dominate the artistic life of New York. Of the friends of Newman's own generation most sympathetic to him, William Morris Hunt died in 1879, shortly after completing his murals at Albany, and William Babcock had settled at Barbizon, too far away for direct communication.

Newman stayed in New York through 1880, when he was living at 64 Washington Square, but in the spring of 1881 he was back at Clarksville. His association with the young painters of New York, however, had been reinforced before his return to Tennessee. Wyatt Eaton, who had spent four years in France, dividing his time between Paris, where he studied under Gérôme, and Barbizon, where he had befriended Millet, returned to New York in 1876. Twenty-two years younger than Newman, Eaton nevertheless became his intimate friend.

Although Newman reached the age of fifty in 1877, his stay in New York during the 1870s marks the true beginning of his career. He no longer had to be occupied, as he had been at Clarksville and Nashville, in attempting to create a favorable climate in which to live and in having to paint portraits to support himself. The grandiose notions of life-size, full-length portraits and heroic battlescenes were left behind. He had entered into the most vigorous art climate of the day and had found colleagues sympathetic to his work. He did not, however, participate in their efforts to reform their professional life or in their exhibitions. He showed only once in the annual exhibitions of the Society of American Artists, when in 1899 Daniel Chester French submitted one of his

18. *The Holy Family*, cat. no. 25.

works. He had escaped the style of painting "born of that benign mother of the 'American school' Düsseldorf," as William Brownell, in 1880, described works acceptable to the National Academy.[32] His color and the vigorous brushwork he had inherited from Couture found favor among the young artists opposing the Academy. He needed no further incentive to work.

Needless to say, Newman was unhappy at Clarksville after his New York experience. Sometime around 1880, he had put up for sale at Doll and Richards, art dealers of Boston, two paintings, a head by William Morris Hunt and an unidentified subject by

19. *Madonna and Child*, 1897, cat. no. 30.

20. *Madonna and Child,* cat. no. 32.

Charles Monginot, which he now asked to have put "in the first suitable auction of pictures in Boston." "I shall remain here," he wrote from Clarksville on October 1, 1881, "until these pictures are sold, and have not determined where I shall go." He added that the summer had been a long one, "five months of hot weather," and that "the principal subject of interest here is the effect of the drouth on the crops, the rise in the price of provisions. This country is but little interested in the fine arts, after the meat and bread question is settled millinery and going to church have place."[33]

21. *Evensong*, cat. no. 168.

Return to Barbizon

The sale of Newman's pictures at Boston brought him 800 dollars.[34] Additional moneys raised by Wyatt Eaton through sales of Newman's works to the editors of *Century Magazine* enabled him to join the exodus of American artists to Europe in 1882. Weir, Albert P. Ryder, and the sculptor Olin L. Warner were among the younger New York artists who returned to Europe that year; Eaton joined their ranks during the following year. They did not travel together, but their purpose was the same: they sought to renew their work at the source.

On this third trip abroad, Newman once again visited his friend Babcock at Barbizon, spending some months there. The many vestiges, for such they are, of the Barbizon influence that have been seen in his work undoubtedly stem from this time.[35] Newman, however, had little interest in landscape painting as such. He "loved fine trees," as Nestor Sanborn had pointed out, and there are a number of drawings to attest to that love (figs. 21 and 22). He also "loved to watch the vivid drama of the skies."[36] Nevertheless, as Sanborn puts it, he "felt, justly, that while Nature was the great basic fact that mere transcription was not the real artist's work"; the artist must "select and combine . . . Nature unalloyed was more often wrong than right."

The Barbizon painters had all passed on by 1882. Newman, how-

22. *Trees,* cat. no. 192.

ever, was certainly familiar with their work. He had met Millet in 1854 and was one of the first Americans to buy a Millet canvas. The trees of Théodore Rousseau, the fields of Millet, the landscapes of Corot and Narcisse Diaz were known to Newman, not only from their paintings, but from direct observation of the scenes from which they were drawn. There is little doubt that his view of the countryside around the village of Barbizon was colored by the Barbizon painters' depictions of it, as their views were colored by one another's.

Newman viewed the landscape as an adjunct to the dramas he depicted. In this, he differs greatly from Corot and Diaz, for example, to whom the landscape itself is often the drama and the figures mere adjuncts to it. He differs also from Millet, to whom the landscape is part of the reality of the story he tells. Newman translated one Millet canvas into his own terms. The Millet, *Sheep at the Edge of Wood* (fig. 25, present location unknown), reads almost like a photograph of an actual scene with as much emphasis given to the trees as to the sheep. Newman, obviously struck by the way the light strikes the flocking of the sheep at the left of the picture, emphasizes that action. In bold masses of lights and darks, all attention is centered on them, as if their sole purpose is to illustrate the simile "like sheep": the landscape simply serves to dramatize the action (fig. 26). Another translation by Newman, that of Eugène Delacroix's *Good Samaritan* of 1852 (Victoria and Albert

23. *Woodland Companions*, cat. no. 156.

Museum, fig. 27), clearly shows how Newman subordinated the landscape to the dramatic presentation of his subjects. Delacroix, like Millet in the *Sheep at the Edge of Wood*, gives as much emphasis to the details of the landscape as to the figures he portrays and even depicts the ass as a third party in the drama, although the ass is a neutral figure in the action of the moment. In the Newman (fig. 28), the lushness of the Delacroix landscape becomes a bleak mass into which the ass fades; all emphasis is on the compassionate gesture of the Samaritan.

The love of trees and of the vivid drama of the skies never led Newman, as it did many of the Barbizon painters and their followers, into an essentially pantheistic view of the world.

Return to New York

Newman remained in Europe for less than a year before returning to New York, which was to be his home for the remainder of

24. *Woodland Companions*, cat. no. 158.

his life. It is not certain where he first lived on his return, but sometime during the 1880s he moved into the modern Benedict Chambers, 80 Washington Square East, with his young friend Wyatt Eaton, who "looked after his welfare in all possible ways."[37] Eaton, a man of poetical temperament, had been one of Millet's intimates, and in 1883 returned to Barbizon for a two-year stay. It is quite possible that he surrendered his studio to Newman during his absence, and it is certain that Newman lived with him after his return in 1885 or 1886. Samuel A. Chapin, who at the time assisted Mary Mapes Dodge in the editing of *St. Nicholas Magazine*, recalls that his rooms at the "Benedick," as it was affectionately called by the many bachelors who lived there, "adjoined those of the late Wyatt Eaton, who, out of the greatness of his heart, had taken Mr. Newman under his protecting wing and cared for him like a devoted son." Chapin added that Newman "was then a very old man, as irresponsible as a child in all practical matters, but with an appealing sensitive poet's face that awakened all one's better nature and sympathies."[38]

25. Jean François Millet. *Sheep at Edge of Wood.* Location unknown.

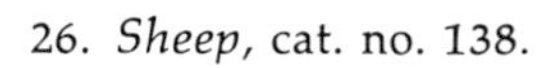

26. *Sheep,* cat. no. 138.

27. Eugene Delacroix. *The Good Samaritan,* 1852. Victoria & Albert Museum.

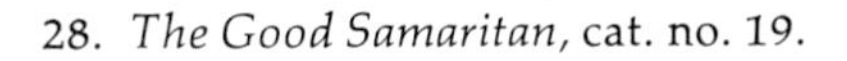

28. *The Good Samaritan,* cat. no. 19.

Albert P. Ryder, Julian Alden Weir, and Olin L. Warner were among the young artists living at the Benedict during the eighties, and at Eaton's studio "foregathered men of such pregnant names as John La Farge, Augustus Saint-Gaudens, Will H. Low, not to mention others to whom American art owes an important debt."[39]

Moreover, Eaton's wide circle of friends included not only his colleagues in the world of art, but men of prominence in the literary and business worlds of the day, most of whom were his contemporaries. It was this world, so to speak, that adopted Newman.

Wyatt Eaton was an intimate of the Gilders, and Newman's first patrons in New York were members of the editorial staff of *Century Magazine* working under the editor-in-chief, Richard Watson Gilder (1844–1909). They included Alexander W. Drake (1843–1916), the art editor; Clarence Clough Buel (1850–1933), associate editor; Robert Underwood Johnson (1853–1937), who succeeded Gilder as editor-in-chief; and Roswell Smith (1829–1892), who, with J. G. Holland, had founded *Century Magazine* (originally *Scribner's Monthly*) in 1870. Mrs. Gilder and Gilder's sister Jeannette (1849–1916), who with her brother Joseph founded the influential magazine *The Critic* in 1881, also bought Newman's works, as did many of the Gilder's friends, among them Stanford White (1853–1906), the architect; William Merritt Chase (1849–1916), the painter; and Henry Blake Fuller (1857–1929), the author.

In addition, a number of the most prominent collectors and connoisseurs of the day, all of the same younger generation and all of Eaton's circle of friends, purchased Newman's paintings. They included John Gellatly (1853–1931), Thomas B. Clarke (1848–1931), Theron J. Blakeslee (d. 1914), William T. Evans (1843–1918), and Sir William Van Horne (1843–1915). John Gellatly offered the greatest support; he is reputed at one time to have owned thirty paintings by Newman.[40]

The situation is an extraordinary one. Artists generally find their greatest support among their contemporaries and are too often ignored by the generation immediately succeeding their own.

Newman's work, however, was little known outside this select group of his admirers. He did exhibit a *Little Red Ridinghood and the Wolf* (probably fig. 29) in the fifth autumn exhibition of the National Academy of Design in 1886, but it is doubtful that it attracted much attention. This situation was corrected in 1894, when Stanford White, Francis Lathrop, Henry Blake Fuller, William Merritt Chase, Alexander W. Drake, Robert Underwood Johnson, and John Gellatly assembled 109 of his works for an exhibition at the Knoedler Gallery at 170 Fifth Avenue. The exhibition, held from the first to the fifteenth of March, was the only showing of Newman's work held during his lifetime. The names of thirty-nine lenders are listed in the catalog of the exhibition. John Gellatly lent fourteen paintings, Miss A. D. Kittell, nine; Francis Lathrop, nine; Robert Underwood Johnson, seven; Sir William Van Horne, four; and Alexander W. Drake, four. Other lenders included T. J. Blakeslee, Clarence C. Buel, William Merritt Chase, Samuel A. Chapin, the stained-glass worker Otto Heinigke, the architects Henry J. Hardenburgh and Charles I. Berg, and many others.

The catalog was introduced with a brief biographical note on Newman and the following statement:

Mr. Newman's pictures are in oils, and are, for the most part, small, and include a number of variations on the same theme. His canvases are never seen at the exhibitions, but have been privately sold, and are widely scattered, and the present collection is designed to give the public for the first time an idea of the rare qualities of a too little-known painter, who has lived in New York for many years in retirement, almost in seclusion. The collection will comprise not only pictures lent for the purpose, but a few examples for sale, in all over a hundred frames.

Fourteen paintings were sold from the exhibition, and the names of Charles T. Yerkes of Chicago and George A. Hearn of New York were added to the list of prominent collectors of Newman's work.[41]

The exhibition was well received. The reviewer for *The Critic* noted that the exhibition "will make it hereafter impossible truthfully to complete the list [of living American... colorists of rare beauty, such as La Farge and Inness], without including the name of R. L. Newman." Of Newman's paintings, he wrote:

To say that Mr. Newman's work reminds us of Delacroix, Monticelli, Diaz and Millet, is to pay it the highest compliment. What other of our American painters reminds us agreeably of the color of the masters? Many of them suggest one another, but Mr. Newman's individuality is not eclipsed by his affiliations. He exhibits that rare and delightful characteristic which we call quality, and which the world cherishes equally with power. It makes little difference what is the subject of his pictures—a "Madonna and Child," a "Hagar and Ishmael," a "Good Samaritan," a "Red Riding-Hood," a "Sappho," a tiger or a group of children— and these are recurring themes—what one feels first is the sincerity and brilliance of his color on a poetic background of mysterious tones. He handles color not timidly, but with an almost spiritual perception of its pervasiveness in nature. He has nothing of the exactness of the topographical school that can map the very mist; but he adds to nature the subtle indefinable but indispensable ideality that makes it art.[42]

In a similar vein, a writer for the *New York Tribune* noted:

If Mr. Newman is to be discussed with reference to any foreign masters at all, he is perhaps best described as a compound of Monticelli and Diaz, with a hint of Delacroix occasionally making itself felt. The beautiful painting of

29. *Little Red Ridinghood,* cat. no. 99.

Christ Lifting St. Peter from the Waves [fig. 31] *recalls distinctly some of Delacroix's sacred sea-pieces. But this very picture will serve as well as any less reminiscent of another hand to illustrate the essentially original elements in Mr. Newman's art. He is before all a colorist, and after that an improvisatore, creating fanciful pictures of generally poetic drift rather than of specifically dramatic or imaginative significance. The composition of the religious picture just referred to is obscure in details, and not specially ingenious in mass, but the atmosphere that fills the piece is undeniably mysterious and poetic. . . .   Mr. Newman's color strikes the*

30. *Hagar*, cat. no. 23.

deep, resonant chord which began with the Venetians and was revived, somewhat thinned but still warm and vivid by Diaz and Monticelli. Like Diaz, the American painter seems to use his subject chiefly as an excuse for an arrangement of color, but Mr. Newman's mood is always elevated, and there is nothing artificial or sophisticated about his work . . . in the main, you feel that Mr. Newman's imaginative conceptions were arrested on their way into concrete images by a flood of light and color too bewitching to let the constructive faculty of the artist have free play. He pauses to weave dreams with the magic of deep purples, glowing reds and soft, forest-like greens. It is a magic of which it would be impossible to deny the potency in his sensitive hands.[43]

Following the exhibition at Knoedler's, eighty-seven of the paintings were sent to Boston to be shown at the Museum of Fine Arts from March 27 to April 17. Newman's reception at Boston was as warm as it had been in New York. Under the influence of William Morris Hunt, however, some Bostonians had perhaps had their fill of the Barbizon painters; to them any suggestion of Barbizon was something of an anathema. One critic went so far as to write:

31. *Christ Lifting Saint Peter from the Waves,* cat. no. 9.

His work is a reflection of Diaz, Couture, Millet and Delacroix. It is, however, a reflection in a very dim mirror, and it is distinguished by a painful amateurishness. The coloring has a sort of crude semblance of luminosity; of drawing the artist knows next to nothing. There is a sort of poetic feeling, which, however, does little to mitigate the slovenly muddling and fumbling of pigment to an appalling degree of unskilfullness.[44]

The critic who reviewed the exhibition for the *Boston Sunday Herald* found:

The influence which predominates in his work is not so much that of the painters of Barbizon as that of Delacroix, whose style and color are closely imitated in many of his best canvases. To say that a painter strongly reminds one of Delacroix of course implies that he has a wonderful sense of color and the more Newman's little pictures are studied the more fascinated and stirred will one be by this extraordinary and ringing quality of deep and powerful color. That there is nothing original about the work it would perhaps be going too far to say, but it is certain that there is a striking and unmistakable souvenir of Delacroix, of Millet, of Diaz, in turn, in the various examples. Behind all the surface characteristics, however (characteristics which never suggest any inferior artist), the artistic temperament of the man makes itself felt . . . . Immensely decorative and eye-filling, these small canvases are saturated with genuine and touching art sentiment; and with all their defects of draughtsmanship, they are the kind of pictures that no true amateur can resist, that grow upon acquaintance and that become precious household friends to those who live with them.[45]

All the newspaper accounts of the exhibitions in New York and Boston carefully noted that Newman, as the *New York Tribune* phrased it, "is a painter who has for many years remained unknown to the public, but has been appreciated and admired by a small circle of artists and collectors." That circle became enlarged during the 1890s to include a number of friends who were to look after Newman for the remainder of his life, notably the sculptor Daniel Chester French (1850–1931) and the banker Nestor Sanborn (1843?–1936?) and Sanborn's wife, Caroline (1843?–1934), who was an artist. Wyatt Eaton, on whom Newman had been dependent, had left

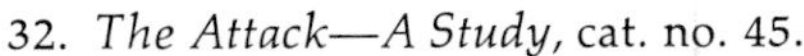

32. *The Attack—A Study*, cat. no. 45.

New York to spend two years (1892 and 1893) in Canada. Newman moved into the famous old Studio Building at 51 West Tenth Street, where William Merritt Chase and many of Newman's other friends lived. Eaton died in 1896 in his forty-seventh year, and by that time French had begun to show an interest in Newman.[46] According to Mrs. French,

Mr. French used to go to see him often on Sunday mornings and sometimes took him a bottle of whiskey or wine. His interest in him was much more in his art than in his personality. He used to say sometimes that he thought Newman cared but little for anybody. . . . Of course, Mr. French admired his painting extravagantly. He said that Newman had all the rare qualities that were lacking in most of the "better painters" and more of the useful practical ones which the successful men all lack.[47]

French himself said of Newman:

It has always seemed to me that it was merely a freak of fortune, or misfortune, that Newman's name was not a household word. As a colorist, it seems to me, that he was very remarkable, and he might easily have become the vogue as so many men of less ability have been. He was an artist through and through, with I regret to say, a good many of the shortcomings that are associated with that name.[48]

For years, French gave Newman a generous monthly allowance. "At one time," he wrote, "a little club was formed, the members of which undertook to contribute so much a month to his support with the understanding that occasionally a picture of his would be awarded to them in recognition of their gifts." He added, "The members gradually fell away until there were only one or two left."[49] French did not name the members of the club, but it is reasonable to believe that Alexander W. Drake and Robert Underwood Johnson were among them; their interest in Newman continued over a period of many years.

Mrs. Drake once wrote that during Newman's late years, "Mr. Drake and some of the other friends felt he needed care and attention, they arranged for him to go to a nice 'home' at Yonkers, I think, and fitted him out with clothes to last through the winter, but he stayed there only one night and went back happily to his own ways."[50]

According to Nestor Sanborn, Newman "had no faculty for business, rather depending instead on friends like Wyatt Eaton to do the unthankful task of placing them [his paintings]." Sanborn wrote that "in later years this job fell into the hands of Mrs. Sanborn and myself and my wife made two exhibitions for him realising several hundred dollars but instead of conserving his little capital he would be off to Europe with high imaginations only to write us that he was strapped and must be brought back again."[51]

For many years Mrs. Sanborn had a studio in Bible House in Astor Place, New York City, where she taught privately and where her artist friends gathered.[52] In 1908, and again in 1909, she offered Newman's work for sale at exhibitions she mounted in her studio, and Newman did indeed set out for Europe after each of the two sales, although he had passed his eightieth birthday. In 1908, he first visited London, taking quarters in Chelsea, and then, at the invitation of the sculptor Andrew O'Connor (1874–1941), spent some time at Clamart, outside Paris, where O'Connor offered him a small house in his garden. Mrs. O'Connor recently recalled that "he brought a supply of Kentucky whiskey, later he took to our wine, only the best would he touch." She remembers "that he was spoiled, demanding, and very hard to live with."[53]

O'Connor, who had been a pupil of Daniel Chester French's, had done a bust of Newman some years earlier in New York. In 1908, he showed it at the Paris Salon and it was purchased by the French government. Newman wrote to Sanborn that he was now on a perpetual "bust" in Paris.

In 1909 he again went to London, but, in Sanborn's words, "advancing years have rubbed the bloom away; nothing suits him—not even the once delectable bitter ale."[54]

Newman continued to live at the Tenth Street Studio Building until 1900, when he moved to 250 West Fourteenth Street, where he took "a hall-bedroom studio," as it was described by one of his visitors, with "a Bible and a dictionary on his mantel and his blanket folded on the floor."[55] By 1906, he had moved into a studio at 119 East Twenty-third Street which, Sanborn said, "was as bare of properties as a barn, 3 chairs a table for his books & papers his easel and a clear burning coal fire were his delight."[56] Newman always slept on the floor, according to Sanborn, because "his asthmatic difficulties would not admit of a bed." On his return from his last trip abroad in 1909, he moved into a roominghouse at 243 President Street, Brooklyn.

During these late years of his life, Newman continued to paint. As Sanborn has noted, it was his habit to "paint a couple of hours each morning and read during afternoons and late into the night."[57] According to Sanborn, Newman was a "profuse tho not a profound reader and confined his reading to the humorous parts of Dickens, Scott, and was very well read in Roman & Greek history."

Nestor Sanborn has described Newman "as hearty simple honest and naive and shrewd withal."[58] Physically, "he was of good figure and had a skin as fair and lovely as a babe's." He had "quite a distinction of manner" and was "an immaculately clean man." Moreover, "he was the youngest and jolliest old man" that Sanborn had ever known "and his spirit was young to the last." Although "he loved all good things, none better, and was as good a judge of a bottle of Pommard as he was of a picture," during his late years "he had small use for things." In 1900, when Newman was in his seventy-third year, his friend Clara MacChesney (1860?–1928) painted his portrait, in which he is shown seated at a table, holding a mug in one hand. Newman called it the "two mugs." The portrait shows his pink, fair skin, set off by white hair and a full white beard. A wise, almost cynical smile finds expression in the eyes and mouth; Newman is obviously enjoying himself.[59]

Clara MacChesney and Andrew O'Connor represent still another "later generation" of artists–those born around 1870–who befriended Newman. The painter Albert L. Groll (1868–1952) and the sculptor Augustus Lukeman (1872–1935) are to be counted among this group.

On March 30, 1912, at the age of eighty-five, Newman moved from Brooklyn to 206 East Eighteenth Street, Manhattan, where he took a room on the ground floor. He arrived "with little . . . in the way of baggage–a few old picture frames, a straw valise, a shawl strap and six paintings."[60] Daniel Chester French, who saw him that morning, said he was "in the best of spirits . . . planning for the sale of some of his pictures."[61] The next morning he was found dead of asphyxiation by gas escaping from a heater. Wallace Sawyer, who, according to Sanborn, was Newman's "most intimate and dearest friend"[62] at the time, came to call and, finding the door blocked and smelling gas, had the police break into his room: Newman, who always slept on the floor, had pushed the bed against the door. On his easel "stood an almost complete desert scene," which Sawyer recognized "as one Mr. Newman had been working on with great interest." Evidently he had worked on it late into the night and had lain down on the floor, fully clothed, to rest; he appeared to be asleep.[63] A light still burned in the room.

Little remained to be done. Sanborn has described the simplicity of the final arrangements: "Wallace Sawyer took charge of all expenses of his funeral leaving Mrs. Sanborn the details of last duties, i.e., the meeting of a few friends at his bier, the incineration of his remains, and the disposition of his ashes beside the remains of his mother."[64] Newman's ashes are buried at the foot of his mother's grave in Riverview Cemetery, Clarksville, Tennessee.

The administrator's sale of Newman's estate was held at the Fifth Avenue Art Galleries on June 6, 1912, with James P. Silo as auctioneer. The estate comprised ten paintings, one of which may have been the "desert scene" on which Newman last worked. The only known work of Newman's that could be called a desert scene is his *Hagar* (fig. 30), presented to the Metropolitan Museum of Art, New York, by Wallace Sawyer's widow in 1925. The title *Hagar* does not appear in the catalog of the 1912 auction, but two

33. *Christ Stilling the Tempest,* cat. no. 11.

works, both listed as *Landscape and Figures* are of the same dimensions as the *Hagar,* which may well have been one of them, and it is reasonable to assume that Wallace Sawyer would have purchased it. *Hagar* is a tragic picture, a foreboding of rejection, if not of death, in which Ishmael is depicted at a distance from his mother. The light of a crescent moon is all that illuminates the scene. The angel of the Lord has not yet appeared.

II NEWMAN AND RYDER

Effort has recently been made to link the work of Albert Pinkham Ryder to that of Robert Loftin Newman.[65] That the two men knew one another is a matter of record. They often met at Mrs. Sanborn's studio in Bible House, they shared in the patronage of a number of the same collectors and dealers, and they enjoyed in common the friendship of many of their peers. John Gellatly, Thomas B. Clarke, William T. Evans, Theron J. Blakeslee, Sir William Van Horne, Daniel Cottier, James S. Inglis, Charles Erskine Scott Wood, and William Macbeth can be counted among their patrons. Wyatt Eaton, Francis Lathrop, Clara MacChesney, William Morris Hunt, John La Farge, and Albert Groll were among their artist friends.

Both Newman and Ryder came under the influence of Thomas Couture. Newman, as has been pointed out, studied with Couture in Paris in 1850. Ryder, however, had no direct contact with Couture. He came under his influence through his first teacher, William E. Marshall, who studied with Couture during the 1860s. Wyatt Eaton, the friend of both Newman's and Ryder's, had met Marshall in the 1860s, and according to G. W. Sheldon, Marshall's "suggestions and sympathy greatly inspirited and otherwise benefited him."[66] Marshall was not a very accomplished painter, but was apparently a sympathetic friend. He is best known today for his portraits, but as Lloyd Goodrich notes, he "painted some romantic and religious subjects that makes one understand why Ryder was attracted to him" and why Marshall remained his "friendly critic for some time."[67]

Newman, of course, also painted religious and romantic subjects, and was more skillful in drawing and painting than either Marshall or Ryder. He not only had absorbed Couture's method of drawing his subjects and massing the shadows of his compositions in monochrome before applying his color in economically and often rapidly applied scumbles and glazes, but had the technical facility the method required and the eye to bend it to his own purposes.

Ryder had no such facility. He worked and reworked his canvases, often over a period of years, altering the shapes of his masses until, as one writer put it, "the stability and harmony of masses [was] attained."[68] He repainted over wet surfaces, adding scumbles and glazes at will. Despite all this, he tried to preserve, even to emphasize, the sense of spontaneity, as shown by his bold forms and active surfaces, that is implicit in Couture's method.

It is quite clear that Ryder was more interested in the ends he set out to achieve than in his means of attaining them. Yet, the reflection of Couture's teachings is found in what he had to say about his means. The importance he laid on the stability and harmony of masses is but one of them. He also believed that "it is better to get the design first before I try color."[69] There can be little doubt that such statements are reflections of Couture.

Sometime after 1880, Newman and Ryder both lived at the modern Benedict Chambers in Washington Square East. It is not clear exactly when Newman moved there, but it was probably after his European sojourn of 1882.[70] Wyatt Eaton had helped to finance

34. *The Shipwreck*, cat. no. 139.

that sojourn, and it could well have been Eaton who introduced the two men. In any event, he and Ryder were there at the same time. It was during this time that Newman painted some of his most monumental religious compositions, such as the *Prodigal Son* (fig. 6), *Christ and the Apostles* (fig. 9), and the two versions of the *Good Samaritan* of 1886 (figs. 70 and 75). This was also the time when Ryder turned away from his earlier pastoral subjects to paint such works as his *Pegasus, Christ Appearing to Mary,* and *Jonah,* and the time when Ryder attempted to heighten the color of his palette.

Of the many factors that might account for the emphasis on such subjects at that time, a determining one may have been the great success of John La Farge's murals of the Resurrection, 1877–1878, in the apse of St. Thomas Church, designed by Richard Upjohn and recently built in New York on Fifth Avenue. La Farge, having completed the decoration of Henry Hobson Richardson's Trinity Church in Boston, was in charge of the decoration of St. Thomas. He commissioned Augustus Saint-Gaudens to design the reredos of the altar, and he himself painted the murals on either side of it and directed the design of the stained-glass windows above it. The decorative scheme of the apse and his murals were nothing short of a triumph for La Farge. The murals, destroyed when the church burned in 1905, have long been considered among his finest works.

To the left of Saint-Gaudens's reredos, La Farge painted a *Christ Appearing to Mary* (fig. 35), which, with its figure of Christ draped in the linens of His shroud and the almost prostrate figure of the Magdalen beside Him, in a roadside setting with trees behind the figures, suggest that La Farge based his work on Titian's *Noli me*

35. John La Farge.
Christ Appearing to Mary, 1878.

tangere (National Gallery, London). Ryder's *Christ Appearing to Mary* (fig. 36) and his *Resurrection* (Phillips Collection, Washington, D.C.), both finished by 1885, are slight variations of the same theme. La Farge would certainly have known the Titian, which was acquired by the National Gallery in 1855, and Ryder undoubtedly saw it during his first stay in London in 1877. Newman also painted two versions of the same theme, *Rabboni* (fig. 37) and *Christ and the Magdalen* (fig. 38) but their dates are uncertain. Characteristically, he emphasizes the setting; the road cuts through a densely wooded area. The subject was not one that had engaged other American artists.

To the right of the reredos, La Farge depicted the three Marys at the Tomb; Newman used the same subject in two drawings (figs. 39 and 40) and also did a drawing of the woman of Samaria (cat. no. 193), a theme used by La Farge in his decoration of Trinity Church, Boston.

La Farge had studied briefly with Couture in 1856, and, three years later, went to Newport, Rhode Island, to learn more of Couture's method from William Morris Hunt, who was among the earliest of Couture's students. Moreover, Francis Lathrop, who had stimulated Newman's interest in religious subjects, had been asso-

36. Albert Pinkham Ryder.
Christ Appearing to Mary, ca. 1885.
National Collection of Fine Arts,
Smithsonian Institution.

37. *Rabboni,* cat. no. 39.

ciated with La Farge in the decoration of Trinity Church.

The configuration of events is such that La Farge can be seen as an influence on both Newman and Ryder. At the same time, it is highly improbable that Newman and Ryder, both men of poetic temperament, nurtured by a love of nature, living in close proximity, and moving in the same circle of friends, did not affect one another. Newman, twenty years Ryder's senior and more urbane as well, more skilled as a painter and with a firsthand knowledge of Couture's teachings, had the greater potential of influence. Ryder's change of subject matter as well as his desire to heighten his palette may well have been due to Newman and La Farge, who were, as Sadakichi Hartmann pointed out at the turn of the century, "by far better colorists."[71]

Newman's desire to teach at the college and at the "Male Schools" free of charge while he was living at Clarksville, and his teaching a small class in the public schools of Nashville, which could not have brought him much financial reward, are indications of the pride and pleasure he must have taken in his proficiency in drawing and painting. Hardly less pride and pleasure were to be derived from communicating his skills to a younger colleague.[72]

In addition to *Christ Appearing to Mary,* another subject that engaged both Newman and Ryder, but not other American artists, was *The Lovers.* Newman painted at least five versions of it (fig. 41), and Ryder, one (fig. 42). All probably date from the 1880s. Once again, it is only possible to speculate on whether or not they were engaged on the subject at the same time, or if they drew their subject from the same source. The paintings themselves are the primary documents. All versions, both Newman's and Ryder's, depict a young couple standing close together and facing left. The girl, a head shorter than the man, is nearer the viewer and partly obscures the man. She wears a long gown with a fitted bodice, and he is in doublet and hose and wears an elegant cap of many folds. The similarities between Newman's and Ryder's versions are certainly too great to be a matter of coincidence and suggest that they must have worked from the same source at the same time.

Both Newman and Ryder were friends of the architect Stanford White, who also moved in the Gilder circle. In his art collection, White had a painting, said to be of the Early Venetian School, called *The Lovers,* as described in an auction catalog, in which "a young lady, in a tightly-fitted robe of medieval style, stands half leaning against her lover, who embraces her with one arm around her waist, rests his other hand upon her shoulder, and whispers in her ear. . . . He wears a full-sleeved yellow cloak with high collar, narrow ruff and a red broadcloth cap with intricate folds and tabs."[73]

Efforts to locate the Stanford White painting or a reproduction of it have been unsuccessful, but the description of it is so sur-

38. *Christ and the Magdalen,* cat. no. 8.

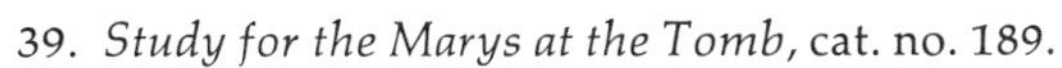

39. *Study for the Marys at the Tomb,* cat. no. 189.

40. *Study for the Three Marys at the Tomb,* cat. no. 190.

prisingly close to what Newman and Ryder painted that it may be considered their source. In Ryder's version, the man appears to whisper to the girl; in Newman's versions, however, with the artist's usual flair for dramatic gesture, he is shown with arm outstretched, pointing the way to a rendezvous. Newman's love of Venetian painting and his eye, attuned to color, would have led him directly to the painting on any of his visits to Stanford White.

In recent years, a small triptych, only 9½ inches high, painted on cigarbox wood—a support often used by Ryder—has come to light. It is a seascape with boats. A common horizon of sky and sea cuts across the three panels. In the center panel, small boats are seen at a distance; in each of the two outer panels, a sailboat in the foreground is silhouetted, in typical Ryder fashion, against sea and sky (fig. 43). The work was apparently done at one sitting from one palette.

Pasted on the back of the triptych is a handwritten inscription, ink on paper, which reads:

Thumbnail sketches by/Albert Ryder and R. L. Newman/ done by special request / for R. L. Newman / 1898 / Property Mrs. R. L. Newman/Murfreesboro, Tenn.

41. *The Lovers,* cat. no. 103.

42. Albert Pinkham Ryder. *The Lovers*. Vassar College Art Gallery, Poughkeepsie, New York. Gift of Mrs. Lloyd Williams, 1940.

The Mrs. R. L. Newman in question was Mattie Todd Newman, who married a Robert L. Newman, a man much younger than Robert Loftin Newman, at Murfreesboro in 1896. She was an amateur painter; her husband did not paint.[74] How she came into possession of the work is not known, and how the triptych reached New York in the 1940s is also unknown. If it is authentic, and there is no reason to doubt that it is, the triptych is a fascinating document of the association of the two men. It could have been painted in either of the artists' studios, or, possibly in Mrs. Sanborn's studio.

The eyes of two different artists are quite apparent in the design of the work. The center panel, with its two boats near the horizon, is so designed that the light striking the sail of one boat is the focal point, and the painting of the sky and the sea, with the light clouds of the one reflected in the other, creates a horizontal rectangle within the vertical panel in such a way as to focus attention on the highlighted sail. This is the eye of Newman, who always centered attention on the highest lights of his canvases. The side panels are designed quite differently, with silhouettes of sailboats accenting the verticality of the panels. This is the eye of Ryder, who invariably exaggerated the rectangular forms of his canvases, whether they were horizontal or vertical.

Newman and Ryder were, of course, very different artists. Although both drew subjects from literature, Newman looked outward, both to nature and to the work of his predecessors, to perceive the part that color plays in our view of the world. Ryder looked inward, to contemplate the mystery of the world. It matters little which was the more proficient, except as one may have aided the other: both achieved their goals.

III NEWMAN'S SUBJECT MATTER

Newman lived a life apart from the world of the professional artist of his time, sharing neither in the activities of the artists of his own generation nor in those of the younger artists who were his chief supporters. He neither submitted his works to the annual exhibitions of his young colleagues, nor did he offer his works in the marketplaces of art. Moreover, he was largely self-taught; the training he had received under Couture was outside the restrictions of academic practice. Throughout his productive years, which is to say throughout his years in New York, he was, insofar as the demands of his profession are considered, a free spirit. The support he received from his colleagues was sufficient for him to protect his freedom by adjusting to a simple mode of life. An essential part of that freedom was the selection of subject matter that best expressed his own feelings about life, without a concern for its commercial value.

Although one may think of the artist of the nineteenth century as being free from the dictates of the aristocratic patronage of earlier years and thus free to pursue his own goals, the dictates of commerce were often more tyrannical than those of the aristocratic

43. Robert Loftin Newman and Albert Pinkham Ryder.
Triptych, 1898, cat. no. 149.

patron. The Paris Salon and its equivalents in other centers of the art world became the major marketplaces of art–so much so that Clarence Cook could write in 1877 that the National Academy in New York "is come to be an establishment for the sale of pictures, and the competition is no longer between artists as to who shall paint the best pictures, but betweeen merchants as to who shall get the best stall in the market."[75] The entrepreneur, who dominates the marketplace today, was only beginning to make his presence felt in Newman's time. The training of the artist was generally entrusted to those who commanded the "best stalls," if for no other reason than the fact that their work was the best known.

The artists who supported Newman, as already noted, were those who set out to reform the education of the artist, as well as the means by which the artist presented himself to the public. It was, without doubt, Newman's freedom of the dictates of the marketplace and of the conventions of any academy that prompted their support of his work.

Newman "loved children, dogs and above all trees" (fig. 44).[76] The children he painted are usually young; often they are infants in their mothers' arms, and the trees under which they are depicted are as protective of them as is the mother, while the dogs are attentive, sometimes playful, companions. The mother and child is the dominant subject of Newman's work, and in his portrayals of the subject, whether religious or secular, the child reaches out, one arm extended, as if to point a way beyond the protective embrace of the mother and the equally protective shelter of the trees (fig. 45).

This gesture of the child is Newman's contribution to the iconography of the mother and child. Other artists have used it as a typical, observed action of a child. But, with Newman, it is a poetic portent of things to come. When he portrays the mother and child with a fortune-teller, in whom the destiny of the child is for the moment invested, the gesture is taken from the child and given to the fortune-teller, and the protective embrace of the mother and the shelter of the trees is threatened (fig. 46).

In two paintings, of the mother and child, *The Nightingale* (fig. 47) and *The Skylark* (fig. 48), the child raises his arm in the direction of the song of the bird. Newman undoubtedly drew such a theme from the romantic poets, for it recalls Keats's *Ode to a Nightingale* and Shelley's *To a Skylark*, both of which deal with man's fate. There would be no joy in hearing the song of the skylark, Shelley writes, "if we could scorn hate, and pride, and fear; if we were things born not to shed a tear." In a similar vein, Keats finds that the song of the nightingale takes us "on the viewless wings of Poesy" away from where "there is no light, save what from heaven is with the breezes blown through verdurous glooms and winding mossy ways."

Newman, of course, is neither illustrating the odes of Shelley or Keats nor interpreting them in any allegorical or symbolic fashion. He is too much the artist for that. He expresses, not in metaphorical or symbolic fashion, but in the terms of his own experience of life on the one hand and in the terms of pure painting on the other, his compassion for the destiny of the child, who is born to shed a tear and who will come to know the light blown from heaven.

In contrast to his portrayal of the mother and child, his portrayals of older children and youths deal with their encounters with the world. In *Children Playing* (fig. 49), or the version of it called *The Mystery* (fig. 50), the children have come upon some inexplicable thing that stirs their imaginations in such a way that it both attracts and repels them. There is nothing in the bleak setting of their little drama to protect them against their fantasies; even the tree to their left seems threatening. Rarely, if ever before, has the imagination of the young been so sympathetically pictured.

Similarly, *The Prodigal Son* (fig. 6) and *The Good Samaritan*

44. *Wood and Figures,* cat. no. 155.

45. *Mother and Child*, cat. no. 105.

46. *The Fortune Teller*, cat. no. 70.

(fig. 70), are set in desolate landscapes, devoid of sheltering trees. The compassion of the Samaritan is shown in his gesture, as he bends over the body of the naked victim. Newman depicted *Sappho* figs. 51 and 52), rejected by her lover Phaon because he loved her not as a woman, but for her genius, seated alone on the barren Leucadian Rock, high above the sea, holding, but not playing, her

47. *The Nightingale,* cat. no. 121.

lyre. Newman underscores the pathos of her realizing that genius isolates her from ordinary mortals.[77] The Magdalen, when comforted by the appearance and words of Christ (fig. 38), is shown under the spreading branches of a great tree; the penitent Magdalen, however, (fig. 53) falls to her knees on barren ground.

Newman strikes a happier note in *The Greek Shepherd* (fig. 54), in which the piping shepherd fills the solitude of his existence with music, and in the *Troubador* (fig. 55)—Newman's only interior scene—in which the musician finds release from confinement in the playing of his lute. In Oliver Goldsmith's novel, *The Vicar of Wakefield,* the daughters of the vicar, Olivia and Sophia, although of marriageable age, are still under the protection of a happy and prosperous family when they consult the gypsy fortune-teller, and

48. *The Skylark,* cat. no. 143.

the gypsy prophesies only the happy ending of their story. There is no indication of the loss of fortune and other trials that the vicar and his family are to undergo before the story ends.[78] Hence, Newman depicts the scene in a sheltered landscape (fig. 56).

The child in *Little Red Ridinghood* (fig. 57) also is innocent of her fate, although in Grimm's version of the tale, which Newman seems to have known, she is forewarned of strangers by her mother. Newman painted several versions of the theme, perhaps because of its special coincidence of child, dog, and trees. The story, once the delight of aristocrats to whom fairy tales were a form of escape, was still popular in the nineteenth century and was used by many artists.[79]

As the critic for the *New York Tribune* pointed out in his review of Newman's 1894 exhibition at Knoedler's, Newman was not primarily an improvisator. He drew his subject matter from many sources; although most of them are from literature, including the Bible, Newman was generally introduced to them through the work of other artists. The use of the mother and child as a subject, in its secular renditions, stems from the Madonna and Child of Christian

49. *Children Playing*, cat. no. 59.

art and became commonplace in Western art during and after the seventeenth century, when it and portrayals of family groups were seen as parallels to the Madonna and Child and the Holy Family.[80] The addition of nimbuses and sometimes of richer color in the draperies is all that distinguishes Newman's religious from his secular versions of the theme. The compositions of *The Holy Family* (fig. 18) and the *Girl and Two Children* (fig. 58) are the same, and Newman's two versions of the theme relating brother and sister, *Brother and Sister* (fig. 59) and *Landscape with Figures* (fig. 60), are variations of the theme of the Virgin and Child.

Newman's depictions of a mother and child seated by the wayside with a fortune-teller, sometimes called *The Fortune Teller* (figs. 46 and 74) and sometimes *The Prophecy* (figs. 61; cat. no. 128), were undoubtedly taken from a version of the same subject painted by William Morris Hunt while Hunt was studying with Couture. Hunt did both a painting and a lithograph of the subject. In its concern with the future of the child, such a depiction can be read as a parallel to the subject of a Rest on the Flight into Egypt. Hunt also painted his *Prodigal Son* while studying with Couture;

50. *The Mystery*, cat. no. 118.

Couture himself painted a version of this parable. The subject matter of the Good Samaritan was undoubtedly known to Newman, not only through the version by Delacroix mentioned above, but through those of Daumier, Millet, J. Alden Weir, and Daniel Huntington.

The portrayal of Olivia and Sophia with the gypsy fortune-teller although taken from one of the most popular novels of the day, also had precedents in painting; Alfred Jacob Miller, for example, exhibited a version of it at the National Academy in 1845.

The list could go on and on. Newman painted a *Girl Bringing Home a New Born Lamb* (cat. no. 78), which was a subject also

51. *Sappho*, cat. no. 136.

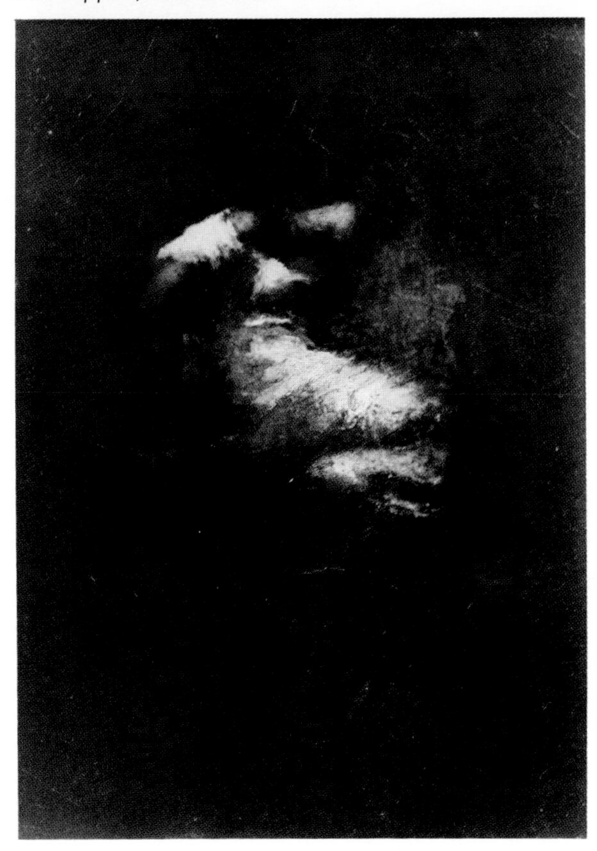

52. *Sappho*, 1875, cat. no. 137.

53. *The Magdalen,* cat. no. 35.

54. *The Greek Shepherd,* cat. no. 83.

55. *A Troubador Playing a Lute,* 1897, cat. no. 150.

56. *The Fortune Teller,* cat. no. 66.

57. *Little Red Ridinghood and the Wolf,* cat. no. 101.

used by both Millet and Hunt. His several versions of *The Bather* (cat. nos. 48–51) reflect Millet's painting of the same subject, as do his several versions of a girl at a spring (cat. nos. 74, 153). His penitent Magdalen (fig. 53), on her knees, with hands clasped, is based on Daumier's painting of the same subject. Newman also took a number of subjects from Delacroix.

Newman does not illustrate in any literal sense the subjects he depicts. There is, for example, no archeological pursuit of detail, so evident in the official art of the nineteenth century. His figures are clothed in timeless draperies or they are naked, and they enact their little dramas in timeless, natural settings. Physiognomic expression, once so dear to the academic world, is almost entirely lacking. Compassion is not measured by time, place, or circumstance, nor is it a passing expression of the features. It is an attribute of human nature, with which Newman identified himself as surely as Delacroix identified himself with human conflict. In both their cases, the subject is nothing less than the vehicle of their experience with life, the intuition of the subjective life apprehended as living intensity.

In portraying his subjects, Newman concentrates all attention on the action of his figures. The settings, although they serve a psychological function, are secondary to the meaning of his subjects. The importance of this emphasis is that it places his work in

58. *Girl and Two Children*, cat. no. 73.

59. *Brother and Sister*, cat. no. 53.

the Latin humanist tradition, outside the pantheistic outlook of so many of the romantic painters of the century, particularly those of Germany and America. There is no preachment, no moral or didactic purpose, and no philosophical implications in his work. His paintings are simple testimonials to the human spirit.

There is much that is autobiographical in Newman's choice of subject matter. Until the death of his mother in his forty-sixth year, he was under her protection, spending most of his time in their home in Clarksville. Hence, the portrayal of the mother as both the protected and protector. He had no father, and in his several portrayals of the Flight into Egypt, Joseph appears almost a phantom figure. His depictions of the male, naked against a bleak world, reflect his life after the death of his mother. *The Prodigal Son* probably refers to his stay in Paris in 1854, when he appears to have squandered borrowed money, and *The Good Samaritan*

60. *Landscape with Figures*, 1903, cat. no. 93.

61. *The Prophecy*, cat. no. 129.

reflects the support offered by such friends as Wyatt Eaton during times of stress. His *Sappho* and *Greek Shepherd* are testimonials to the solitude of the artist.

IV FORM AND COLOR IN NEWMAN'S WORK

Newman has been called "a painter of dreams."[81] As one critic put it, "he weaves dreams with the magic of deep purples, glowing reds and soft forest-like greens."[82] Another speaks of the atmosphere of the dream worlds from which his figures emerge and of "the power of his imagination."[83] Such critical appraisals could be repeated at length and seem to contradict that Newman was not a improvisator. They discount the fact that he drew his subject matter almost exclusively from the work of other artists, subjects that were important to him only as they could serve as genuine vehicles of the expression of his personal experiences. Newman was neither a visionary whose subjects were landscapes of the mind, nor a mystic, whose subjects were symbols of the spirit. If his choice of subjects offers a certain psychological insight into his personality, that is simply because he lived at a time when the artist was free to select his subjects at random, if he chose, as Newman most emphatically did, to avoid the marketplace. Newman's choice of subjects reflects his temperament. Otherwise, his subject matter was more or less the common currency of his time and as such, expresses the sentiment of his time. As Heinrich Wölfflin has so aptly pointed out, however, to take "the history of art as the history of expression runs the risk of disastrous one-sidedness."[84]

What distinguishes Newman's work and makes it of as much interest to us today as it was to his contemporaries, is his use of color. Whatever place his expression may have in the study of his work, it is secondary to the structure that conveys it. In the work of the artist of any persuasion or of any period, it is what distinguishes his particular contribution from that of his colleagues that is important. With Newman, it is not his subject matter, but his use of color.

Color in the ordinary sense of the word is intangible, as dreams are intangible, except to the sense of sight. Hence, Newman's images, structured in color, appeared to his critics as dream images or visions. They are not. To understand that they are not and to understand Newman's use of color, it is first necessary to account for his interest in it and, then, to explain the part color plays in natural philosophy.

62. *Ariadne,* cat. no. 43.

It is clear that Newman was familiar with the writings of Joshua Reynolds. In describing his first visit to the Louvre, for example, he compared his reactions to the masterpieces there with Reynolds's initial reaction to the work of Raphael in the Vatican. Newman's painting *Ariadne* (fig. 62) was based on Titian's version of the same subject in the National Gallery, London, which Reynolds, who stated that "the great end of art is to strike the imagination,"[85] discussed in great detail in his Eighth Discourse (December 10, 1778). In analyzing the Titian, Reynolds emphasized the importance to its composition of the red scarf worn by Ariadne. Newman was evidently attracted to the subject by this analysis; he gave considerable importance to the red drapery he gives to Ariadne in his version of it.

Farther on in the same discourse, Reynolds speaks of how Rembrandt, Correggio, Rubens, Giorgione, and others, used warm colors in their highest lights, and how, instead of discretely describing their figures to give them "a fullness of manner," they described them in relief "by melting and losing shadows in a ground still darker than those shadows." Reynolds then goes on to discuss "those powers over the imagination, which make so very considerable and refined a part of poetry," which the artist has "but scanty means of exciting," adding

It is true, sketches or such drawings as painters generally make for their works, give this pleasure of imagination to a high degree. From a slight undetermined drawing, where the ideas of the composition and characters are, as I might say, just touched upon, the imagination supplies more than the painter himself, probably, could produce.

These aspects of Reynolds's discussion are often forgotten in light of his other, seemingly contradictory statements, but they apparently drew the attention of Newman. It is noteworthy, too, that Reynolds was Delacroix's favorite English theorist,[86] and Delacroix must have been familiar with these passages in Reynolds's Eighth Discourse.

To Delacroix, "form was not a sector of space frigidly cut out by an arbitrary frontier, an outline: it was a mass with a centre of gravity—but turned outwards so as to bathe in the luminous medium into which it had been thrown."[87] Delacroix equated mass with color, and how he achieved that equation was not unlike the method Newman learned from Couture, according to which masses were first "drawn" with a sauce of sepia tint to form the ground of the canvas; colors were then applied over this ground with a loaded brush in such a way that the thickest part of the paint coincided with the highest light of the form, which was also the point nearest the observer; the rest of the form was described by a lighter pressure on the brush, so that its edges melt into the darker mass of the ground beneath them. The resultant form seems actually to curve outward from the ground on which it is painted, much as the forms of a bas-relief project outward from their ground to catch the light. The sense of relief, rather than of a fullness of form, so achieved, is similar to that noted by Reynolds in the work of Rembrandt, Correggio, Rubens, and others, except for the important fact that the form itself is equated with its color. Reynolds spoke only of the warm colors of its highest lights. The difference is well expressed in his journal, *Soi-Même*, by Odilon Redon, who, like Newman, learned much from Delacroix, but, unlike Newman, became a visionary, although he never fully repudiated the natural. Speaking of his teacher Jean Léon Gérôme, Redon wrote, "He ordered me to enclose within a contour a form which, for my part, I saw vibrating." A vibrating form in this sense is one bathed in the luminous medium, light. Redon added, "I feel only the shadows, the visible reliefs, every outline being without doubt an abstraction."[88]

The disavowal of defining a form by its contour and the recognition of the fact that the light in which it is bathed, its color, is what makes the form visible is, to use Reynolds's terms, what allows, from the sketches a painter makes for his works, the imagination of the spectator to supply more than the painter could probably produce. A comparison of any of the sketches of the academicians of the nineteenth century—for example, those by Bouguereau, Cabanel, or Gérôme—with their finished works will bear this out. Of greater significance, however, the rejection of the contour becomes the basic distinction between modern art and the academic. The history of that rejection is a long one and can be traced back at least to the Venetians, but it was Delacroix's equation of form and color that made the contour appear a useless and unnatural convention, an abstraction. Redon could not understand, for example, why Gérôme asked him to close his eyes in order to see.

On the pretext of simplification (and why?) he made me shut my eyes to light and neglect the vision of substances. I have never been able to force myself to do this![89]

Delacroix's intuition of the equivalence of mass and color is accepted by most historians as pivotal to the development of modern art in France. Furthermore, it lies at the heart of the acceptance of the sketchlike finish of a work, simply because the sketch does not constrain the vibrancy of color, and thus the vigor of the form, by defining its contours, nor does it conceal the brushmarks of the artist, which are a characteristic of the sketch. All sorts of esoteric explanations, taken from literature and philosophy, have been put forward to account for this, but the painter's point of view is well stated by the visionary Redon, who put "the logic of the visible at the service of the invisible,"[90] when he called the contour of a form an "abstraction."

The outlining of the contour of a form, together with the laws of linear perspective, is a linear conception that was once useful. It had to be discarded when the study of color began to dominate the work of the artist. The rift between the academician and the modern artist was, in fact, essentially a rift between those who defined masses by their colors and those who attempted to perpetuate their definition by line. The change of outlook by the modern artist, although it was a change from the tactile to the optical in the Wölfflinian sense, was not merely a change from the linear to the painterly. It was a new understanding of the structure of the perception of natural phenomena and hence a new form of description for the artist.

As opposed to the development of modern art in France, the work of Delacroix had little influence in America. Delacroix's name is rarely mentioned in the histories of American art, and it is only since 1930 that any significant exhibitions of his work have been mounted in this country. Newman is one of the few, if not the only American artist of the nineteenth century to understand Delacroix's achievement. John La Farge was on the side of Delacroix in the Delacroix-Ingres discussions, which dominated the Parisian art world when he was in Paris during the 1850s, but there is scant evidence of any influence of Delacroix on his work. When Newman's work was presented to the public in 1894, all critical references to it quite rightly associated it with the work of French artists from Delacroix to Millet. Only one reviewer noted its affiliation with the work of other Americans, namely Inness and La Farge. When Sadakichi Hartmann wrote his *History of American Art* (1902), he was hard put to relate the work of Newman to that of other American colorists and was able to suggest only La Farge

63. *The Miraculous Draught of Fishes,* cat. no. 181.

and Babcock, and even when he revised the work in 1932 he could only add the names of [Frank L.?] Kirkpatrick, William Gedney Bunce, and Maurice Prendergast.

What Newman learned from Delacroix was to construct his figures *par les boules,* as Delacroix called them. *Les boules* were ovoidal planes of color, like sections of the surfaces of spheres, of varying sizes, applied rapidly with the brush to describe those parts of a figure that project into the light toward the observer. Delacroix's pupil and one-time assistant Louis de Planet called them Delacroix's ovals. Couture's method of applying colors over a "sepia" tint, which Newman understood, made it easy for him to grasp both the significance and the practice of this way of constructing figures. It was a way that eliminated defined contours and preserved the vitality of color. Newman also learned from Delacroix to confine *les boules* to the principal figures of his compositions, so that the figures themselves would appear to project in relief from their backgrounds.[91]

This practice of drawing with the brush in color requires skill in draughtmanship. That Newman had the skill is evident from the few drawings of his that are known today. Newman drew much as he painted, that is, in terms of light. His figures are defined less by their contours than by the way the light falls on them, setting them off in relief against their backgrounds. This method can be seen in *The Miraculous Draught of Fishes* (fig. 63), in which lines articulate only those parts of the bodies that are in shadow; the lights merge with the white ground of the paper. His drawings can be likened to negatives of his painted works, in which, conversely, the shadows merge into their darker backgrounds. Delacroix drew in a similar way.

The positive-negative relationship of Newman's paintings to his drawings can be seen clearly in a comparison of his painting of the *Mother and Child* (fig. 64) and his drawing of the same subject (fig. 65). The shadows of the figures in the painting melt and are lost in the deeper shadows of the ground on which they are painted; whereas the lights of the figures in the drawing melt and are lost in the white ground of the paper.

Sometimes, as in the *Mother and Child* mentioned above, Newman emphasized the luminosity of his lights by a mere suggestion of a line between them and the dark background. This was a device also used by Delacroix and Couture.

A few weeks before his death, Delacroix wrote in his notebook, "The first merit of a picture is to have been made for the eye."[92]

64. *Mother and Child*, cat. no. 110.

65. *Mother and Child in a Landscape*, cat. no. 182.

He believed "that painting is made for the sake of being felt and lived, not of being explained." The idea was not a new one, but the new intensity given to it by Delacroix in his use of color affected the course of modern art. Newman not only felt the intensity, but understood the means of attaining it. He became an early advocate of pure painting in America.

The Meaning of Color

Newman selected his subjects from the works of other painters and translated them into the terms of art he had come to comprehend. Although his selection of subjects offers a certain psychological insight into his temperament, as is also the case with Delacroix's selection of subjects, it is meaningless to give them any other interpretation. Newman, like Delacroix, was not an author's painter, but a painter's painter. It should not be overlooked in this context that Delacroix could not tolerate Baudelaire and did not appreciate the interpretation of his work that Baudelaire relayed to the general public.[93] To understand only what Newman expressed, at the expense of neglecting what gave vitality to that expression, is to be guilty of the disastrous one-sidedness against which Wölfflin warned the historian, on the one hand, and which led the critic Thoré, on the other, to conclude that the unanimous approval given to Couture's *Romans of the Decadence* because of its subject matter was an unhappy moment for Couture.

The true meaning of Newman's work is to be found in his comprehension of the meaning of color to our understanding of the structure of natural phenomena. The exploration of color by the French artists of the nineteenth century not only parallels their return to the study of nature, well expressed by Paul Cézanne in his desire to do Poussin over after nature, but also had the effect of eliminating the anecdote from the work of art, reversing the inferior position of landscape and still-life painting in the academic hierarchy of subject matter, a reversal that led eventually to the acceptance of nonobjective, abstract art as pure art.

However esoteric it may sound to unfamiliar ears, there is a relationship between knowledge of the physical reality and the work of art. Until modern times, this relationship was well understood. One needs only to go back to the writings of Leon Battista Alberti and Leonardo da Vinci, both Renaissance men of universal genius, to understand that it was the relationship of art to natural philosophy that placed the fine arts among the liberal arts, and thus elevated the social status of the artist from the position of an anonymous craftsman that he held during the Middle Ages to that of a member of an academy. That position was maintained until the nineteenth century. There are many reasons for its collapse, but the overriding reason was the failure of the academy to recognize that knowledge, either in art or physics, is not static. The chief opponents of the academy were, of course, the artists in France who had returned to the study of nature in their explorations of color; they were the same artists who turned to the painting of landscapes and still lifes, who eliminated the anecdote from painting, and who opened the way to so-called abstract art.

The study of color dominates both the work of the artist and the physicist during the nineteenth century. It had little meaning to either the art or the science of the Renaissance. The great student of Renaissance art Bernard Berenson found that "colour is less essential [than other factors] in all that distinguishes a master painting from a Persian rug."[94] Similarly, Giorgio Vasari, the founder of the Accademia del Disegno, when he first published his *Lives* in 1550, omitted all mention of the Venetian painters, although Titian was then in his seventy-third year, and then gave them slight consideration in his expanded, second edition of the work in 1568, saying, "He who can draw need not rely on color alone to hide the lack of design as many of the Venetians do."[95]

Color, of course, has always been a component of art, as it has always been a component of light. It was not, however, until the second half of the seventeenth century, in 1666 to be exact, that it became known through the investigations of Isaac Newton that color is actually a physical constituent of light. Newton's discovery

66. *Girl Blowing Soap Bubbles*, cat. no. 77.

was important in opening the way to the further investigations of the physical nature of light that now pervade all physical theories.

Light, which makes things visible, is itself not visible. It is a known physical fact today that the light to which the human eye is sensitive is known only by the phenomenon of the color resulting from its reflection from the objects it illuminates. The intuition of the French Impressionists, aided by certain color theories that were accessible to them, studied and painted the structure of such natural phenomena.

67. *Head of a Girl,* cat. no. 87.

Denis Diderot (1713–1784) was among the earliest of the critics to recognize that the colors used by the painter had a physical correspondence with color in nature. In words prophetic of the advent of Impressionism, he wrote of Chardin:

Oh! Chardin, it is not white, red, and black that you mix on your palette: it is the very same substance of the objects, it is the air, the light, that you put on the tip of your brush and apply to your canvas.[96]

It is an unwritten law of the history of art that the structure that gives form to expression becomes lost or reinterpreted when its influence is felt beyond its point of origin. The so-called American Impressionists, for example, never grasped the fact that the French Impressionists were concerned with the structure of light and not with the structure of the objects they painted. The American Impressionists, probably because of their academic training, painted the objects. They borrowed certain technical devices from the French, such as the use of colors that would mix optically in the eye and the use of broken brushstrokes, which heightened their palettes and brought color into their shadows. They were mistaken, however, in their notion that structure is a matter of technique alone. They (the Americans) interpreted *plein air* painting as out-

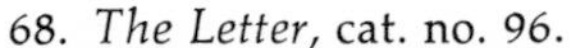

68. *The Letter*, cat. no. 96.

69. *The Flight into Egypt,* cat. no. 17.

door painting, not as the painting of the open air, which disperses the light reflected from objects. That is why one never feels the drift of the air in their work. Similarly, the Italian Futurists saw only the expressive side of the work of the Cubists. Vasari felt the expressive power of the color structures of Titian, but regretted that Titian could not draw like Michelangelo, not realizing that the linear structure, including linear contours, of a work by Michelangelo would not carry, but would indeed subvert the color of a Titian.

That Newman understood the essential structure of Delacroix's work and did not simply borrow certain of his technical devices should be self-evident. His subjects, even when he took them from Delacroix, are of a wholly different nature, expressive of a different temperament. When he borrowed subjects from Delacroix, he tempered them to his own disposition. Despite the fact that Delacroix devoted several paragraphs in his *Journal* (May 7, 1824) to the song of the nightingale, it would be difficult to imagine his painting the subject as Newman did (fig. 47). Nevertheless, it was Newman's understanding of the structure of Delacroix's work that enabled him to project the living intensity of his subjects.

70. *The Good Samaritan,* 1886, cat. no. 21.

Newman, unlike Delacroix in France, had little or no influence on the generations of American artists that came after him. As was the case with Newman in 1850, those generations sought greener pastures than their native soil could offer. The influence of Delacroix came to them through the artists that Delacroix had influenced, particularly through the work of Cézanne and the Cubists, and, more often than not, they attempted to recreate what those artists expressed without understanding the structure of their expression.

The study of color in relation to the structure of perception continued in France from generation to generation. It reached a certain culmination in the work of Cézanne and the Cubists, in which Cézanne's intuition of a geometrical foundation of such perception was decisive.

Cézanne's intuition led him to reconstruct the facts of his observation in terms of a multiplicity of elliptic planes of color which project toward the observer in low relief from the ground of his canvas. As Cézanne himself described them, each of his planes is directed toward a central point and symbolizes a geometrical figure of three dimensions, a cylinder, a cone, or a sphere.[97] The resultant structure is a highly complex one in which one plane represents

71. *Tiger at Rest*, cat. no. 148.

three dimensions, two represent six dimensions, three represent nine dimensions, and so on. These planes of color are the mensurational elements, the building blocks, as it were, of his works. They are geometrical equivalents of Delacroix's "ovals" of color, each of which represents a mass with a center of gravity. Delacroix, however, confined his ovals, as did Newman, to the central figures of his compositions, so that his figures seem to emerge from more or less conventional backgrounds to bathe in the light that illuminates them. Cézanne completely eliminated the traditional idea of the background.

The eye of the observer scans the surface of a canvas by Cézanne at will from plane to plane, and the planes, each directed toward a central point, seem to shift in space as the eye moves from one to another. To emphasize certain of his planes, Cézanne reintroduced the use of lines to mark one or more of their edges, a device also used by Delacroix and Newman. He was most successful at *plein air* painting, where the dispersion of light in the atmosphere seemed to stimulate his eye. His still lifes and figure pieces tend more to the conventional. It remained for the Cubists to analyze objects and figures in the light of their studios.

The structures of Cézanne and the Cubists went far beyond the simple elimination of the contours of figures to preserve the intensity of their colors, and they went far beyond the concentration by Delacroix and Newman on the central figures of their compositions. They were a complete violation of the Renaissance limitation of describing space and events in space by their Euclidean coordinates, line, angle, and volume, and a complete violation of the notion of a fixed point of observation on which the description of the Euclidean coordinates depends. The ovals of Delacroix, so well understood by Newman, are, however, the forerunners of the planes of Cézanne and the Cubists.

The Cubists also referred the structure of their works to geometry. Albert Gleizes and Jean Metzinger wrote in 1912, "If we wished to refer the space of the painters [the Cubists] to geometry, we should have to refer it to the non-Euclidean scientists: we should have to study, at some length, certain theorems of Rieman's [sic]."[98]

The structures of both the physicists and the artists, in which the perception of color—known as energy to the physicists—now plays a dominant role, find their logic in non-Euclidean geometry. The structures of both the natural science and the art of the Renaissance, in which tactile, rather than optical perception played the dominant role, found their logic in Euclidean geometry.[99] Both the Renaissance and the nineteenth century are distinguished by their return to the study of the perception of natural phenomena. The exploration during the nineteenth century of the meaning of color to the structure of expression is one of the most fascinating and challenging chapters in the history of art. The fact that a correspondence can be found today between the work of the physicist and the work of the artist gives assurance that the work of the artist still belongs among the liberal arts as the Renaissance understood them, that it is not merely a matter of technical proficiency on the one hand or of the expression of sentiment on the other. The scientist claims that modern concepts of the physical reality are too complex for visual representation. It is quite possible, however, that the modern artist in his pursuit of the meaning of color to structure has found the key to such representation in the elliptic plane of color. In any event, he has given a true sense of form to the expression of sentiment that transcends time. Certainly Newman's subject matter belongs to the age in which he lived, but it still touches us because of the form in which he cast it.

Newman's role in the development of modern art is certainly a minor one. The outstanding American colorists of later generations, Maurice Prendergast (1859–1914) and Milton Avery (1893–1966), owed nothing to him in the way that the French colorists were indebted to Delacroix. Prendergast lived in France, and Avery, during the formative years of his career, lived in New York at a time when the French moderns were much in evidence. The artists of the generation born around 1850, who supported Newman, were influenced by the academic training of Munich and Paris and by the work of the Pre-Raphaelites. Newman's use of color had little or no effect on their work. They undoubtedly supported Newman because he was not of the Düsseldorf school favored by the National Academy. They simply posited their academic styles against the Academy's; once their styles became acceptable, it was to their benefit to merge with the Academy, which they did.

It was not until after the second World War that American painting, stimulated by the Surrealists who lived in America during the war, and by their spokesmen, Marcel Duchamp and André Breton, gained international status. Abstract Expressionism led the way. It was essentially a passage from Surrealism to abstraction in which the psychological, the expressive, content of the work dominates the structural. Following the Abstract Expressionists, the so-called "color field" painters and "geometric abstractionists" (whose works, incidentally, have little or nothing to do with geometry), were influenced by the successes of their predecessors. Like the Abstract Expressionists, they painted abstract landscapes of the mind, which also emphasized the expressive over the structural.

There is, at present, a revival of interest in the academic art of the nineteenth century and, concurrent with it, an interest on the part of the American artist in a kind of surreal expression based on academic principles. Both interests, in their return to the academic framework of perception, seem to be a reaction against a surfeit of expression that has no reference to the physical reality. As such, it is also an influence of one generation on another.

The situation was different in Newman's day. Generation after generation of American artists were influenced by what was happening in the art centers abroad, as was the case with Newman. Lewis Mumford stated Newman's position in America very well when he wrote:

What was positive and creative in this period usually worked against the grain of its major activities. Its best works were often produced in obscurity, like the paintings of Albert Pinkham Ryder and Robert Loftin Newman, like the poems of Emily Dickinson, or the philosophic reflections of Charles Peirce.[100]

There would be little purpose in bringing Newman's little pictures, "sometimes no larger than a man's hand,"[101] to attention today if they were of antiquarian interest only. In their humble way, they still touch the heart, and they tell us much of the historical development of art in America.

The first work of Newman's to enter a public collection was his *Madonna and Child* (fig. 72). It was presented to the Brooklyn Museum in 1914, two years after the artist's death, by A. Augustus Healy, the president of the museum's board of trustees. Together with eight of Newman's paintings lent by Nestor Sanborn, the *Madonna and Child* was shown in the exhibition "Works by American Painters 1860–1885," which the museum mounted in November 1917 to celebrate the opening of the Catskill Aqueduct. Works dated from 1860 to 1885 were selected because those years, representing the most significant years in the development of New York City's water-supply system, were also seen to represent the movement away from the Hudson River School of landscape painting to the work of "rugged and free individualists who seemed to be reaching out into new fields unknown to their predecessors."[102] Seven of the eight Newmans lent by Sanborn were purchased by the museum. These, with the *Madonna and Child* and three drawings added to the museum's collection, constitute the largest holdings of Newman's work by any museum.

The first appreciation of Newman's work to appear in print after his death was written and published by Frederic Fairchild Sherman in *Art in America* (4 [April 1916]: 177–84). Sherman noted that Newman's color "is developed with all the loving and painstaking care that another artist might have lavished on the drawing of a figure, and simply because he realized that it was a surer means for the expression of what he had to say than any further development of the more obvious detail could be."

The *Brooklyn Museum Quarterly* in 1921 (8 [October 1921]: 157–61) published brief notes on Newman's life, compiled by Nestor Sanborn, along with a critical estimate of Newman's work by Sanborn. The biographical notes are a primary source for the study of Newman, and Sanborn's critical estimate of Newman's work, with which he was certainly more familiar than anyone else has ever been, are far from superficial. He discusses "the momentous change that would ultimately result" from the break with the academic formulas by Delacroix, Daumier, Courbet, and Turner, and how color, "which to the men of the past had been a mere accessory to black and white drawing," began with Cézanne "to near its ultimate significance as a functioning element" in the structure of the work of art. Moreover, he notes that the function of color is "inherent in itself." "Newman," he says, "came at a time when, like Delacroix, he unconsciously absorbed the new movement . . . to form organization in relation to color values and symmetry," and adds:

Mr. Newman's color-vision, like Albert Ryder's poetic expression in pigment, stands absolutely individual and alone,

72. *Madonna and Child,* 1897, cat. no. 27.

and it is in this sense that these two rare types, paradoxically a diverse unity, combine and attain to a distinct status in American art.

The same year that Sanborn published his comments, Mrs. Wallace Sawyer, the widow of Newman's intimate friend, presented two works to the Metropolitan Museum of Art, New York, *Saint John the Baptist* (fig. 73) and *The Fortune Teller* (fig. 74). In 1925, she added a third painting, *Hagar* (fig. 30), to its collection.

The first major exhibition of Newman's work to be held after his death was mounted in April 1924 by the art dealer Frank K. M. Rehn in his New York galleries. A small group had been shown at the Babcock Galleries in New York in 1919, but the exhibition at Rehn's included over thirty paintings. The collector John Gellatly had consigned for sale four Newmans to Rehn in 1919, and they formed the nucleus of the exhibition. So widely scattered were Newman's paintings, however, that it took Rehn four years to locate a sufficient number to mount the exhibition.

Guy Eglington, the English art critic and one-time editor of *International Studio,* "convinced that Newman was one of the most neglected masters in the history of American painting," reviewed the exhibition (*International Studio,* 79 [June 1924]: 228). In his review, Eglington mentioned that he had asked Nestor Sanborn "to write a longer article [than that published in the *Brooklyn Museum Quarterly* three years earlier], which should be published in the *Studio* and should make people sit up." Alas, the article was never written, but Eglington "sounded Newman's trumpet in many ears, but with little success," a circumstance which he attributed to the fact that "no one knew where his [Newman's] works were to be found." As to Newman's place in art, Eglington wrote:

In face of this exhibition, it is impossible to write Newman down as a dilettante. He was in the first place a great colorist. And one has only to glance at the "Good Samaritan" [fig. 75] *or "The Letter"* [fig. 76], *which Mr. Phillips has bought for the Phillips Memorial Gallery, to see that he was more.*

Virgil Barker, the historian of American art, writing in *The Arts* (5 [1924]: 291–92) felt, however, that the Rehn exhibition served only "to bring into greater prominence one of this country's minor artistic talents." Nevertheless, he wrote that Newman "had the intelligence to strive for truly pictorial qualities; he used a palette of rich colors richly blended; he often designed with marked subtlety; and he worked on a small scale, which was suited to his motives and which intensified his virtues as a painter."

Duncan Phillips did indeed buy *The Letter,* mentioned by Eglington, and *The Skylark* (fig. 77), from the Rehn exhibition, but he, too, felt that Newman was a minor artistic talent, calling him "an

73. *Saint John the Baptist*, cat. no. 40.

74. *The Fortune Teller*, cat. no. 69.

75. *The Good Samaritan,* 1886, cat. no. 20.

76. *The Letter,* cat. no. 94.

inadequately equipped amateur who was none the less a very sincere and appealing artist."[103] His purchases, however, added two more Newmans to American public collections, and the Newark Museum's purchase of the *Good Samaritan*, also mentioned by Eglington, from the same exhibition added still another.

After the Rehn exhibition, Newman was again forgotten until 1935, when the Whitney Museum of American Art in New York City mounted an exhibition of fifty-one of his paintings and six of his drawings. The neglect of his work was such that Edward Alden Jewell, writing in the *New York Times* (January 20, 1935), could say, "Robert Loftin Newman may never have been heard of by most of us today." Jewell continued:

The mere digging up of a minor nineteenth century American artist and his presentation to the public as a rescued painter whose work the hurrying world has neglected and forgotten need not necessarily mean very much in itself. But Robert Loftin Newman, even though we continue to feel that he was minor, proves to have been a man of genius, with a fine and

77. *The Skylark*, cat. no. 144.

sensitive appreciation both of the values discernible in human life and of the materials with which an artist is wont to express the vision that is his. . . .

His art is full of understanding: full of an artist's and of a true poet's aspiration. His songs are sung from a heart that feels and schooled to coherence and convincing formal beauty by a mind that thinks and that bases its decision upon art's undying principles.

Jewell's comments on Newman's obscurity and his critical evaluation of Newman's work were characteristic of the response to the exhibition. Lewis Mumford, for example, writing in *The New Yorker* (January 26, 1935), noted three qualities that gave "genuine distinction" to Newman:

His color, to begin with, was rich and personal. . . . In the movement of his figures, he is good enough to recall Delacroix, to whose smaller studies his canvases sometimes bear a surprising resemblance. Above all, he had the power of suggesting detail without having to supply it—paintings like his "Adam and Eve" [fig. 78] *make one think not so much of a sketch—for there is evidence of careful study—as of a great picture seen at a distance.*

The reviews of the Newman exhibitions of 1924 and 1935 inevitably compared Newman's work with that of Ryder. Virgil Barker, for example, noted that "Newman may fairly be said to have possessed more technical resources and variety than Ryder, but the latter triumphs by his greater conceptions." Edward Alden Jewell found "little actual similarity" between the two painters, but, nevertheless, felt compelled to link their names because "in spirit Newman seems close to Ryder." Lewis Mumford felt that Newman's work is "not uniformly so interesting as Ryder's." As a result of such comparisons, M. Knoedler and Company, New York, held a joint exhibition of their works in 1939, with each of the two artists represented by twenty carefully selected paintings.

In general, the response to the direct comparison of the works of the two men brought attention to the superior technical abilities of Newman. An anonymous critic, however, writing in the *Art Digest* (November 15, 1939), was perceptive enough not only to call Newman "an excellent draughtsman who distorted with a sure knowledge of distortion and who loved the mystery of light and color," but to see clearly that "Ryder had different visions, for essentially Newman was a realist." Similarly, James W. Lane, writing in *Art News* (November 11, 1939), associated at least one of Newman's canvases with the work of Fantin-Latour, noting, however, that Newman's palette "sings against the grain of the canvas." Lane added: "Newman carries off the honors in this comparison of work, because, while the ground against which his figures are set has no

78. *Adam and Eve,* cat. no. 1.

less murk than Ryder's, his figures, even when dimly shown, are drawn with an exactitude in color values and shading which is astonishing." Margaret Breuning, writing in *Magazine of Art* (32 [December 1939]: 714–16), concluded that Newman "is a unique figure, significant not only because he could translate familiar themes into magical splendor, but, also, because he possessed rare artistic gifts."

In 1942, Newman was honored as a native-born Virginian artist by the Virginia Museum of Fine Arts in Richmond, which held a memorial exhibition of thirty-seven of his paintings and seven of his drawings. Since then, although his paintings have been seen in a number of group exhibitions, the only one-man showing of his work was at the Graham Gallery in New York City, in 1961, when the thirty-odd paintings collected by the late Joseph Katz of Baltimore were put on view.

The story is one of appreciation when his works are put on view and of neglect when they are taken down. Since the Whitney Museum exhibition of 1935, Newman's name has been included in most histories of American art, usually linked with Ryder's, but without much understanding of his distinct contribution to American art. A lack of familiarity with his works, which are rarely seen, undoubtedly accounts for the lack of understanding of that contribution.

NOTES

1. Robert L. Newman, "Museums of Art: Musée du Louvre," *Nashville Union and American*, December 12, 1872.

2. The letter to Durand was found by Jules Prown among the Durand Papers in the manuscript room of the New York Public Library, and Prown forwarded a photostat of it to Walter Sharp in 1956. Cunningham's "Painters and Sculptors," referred to by Newman, was one of the many editions published in this country of Allan Cunningham's *The Lives of the Most Eminent British Painters and Sculptors*, a multivolume work; Newman's saying that it was the only book on artists that he had read is probably nothing more than an expression of the poverty of art he suffered.

3. Mary Bartlett Cowdrey, *American Academy of Fine Arts and American Art-Union*, 2 vols. (New York, 1953), 2: 267.

4. Nestor Sanborn remains almost as elusive a figure as Newman. He was a resident of Brooklyn and his wife, Caroline, was an artist. Sanborn's notes on Newman's life, published in the *Brooklyn Museum Quarterly* (8 [October 1921]: 157–61) are a prime source for the study of Newman. Guy Eglington tells of meeting Sanborn at the Newman exhibition held by Frank K. M. Rehn in New York in 1924 and describes him as "one of the most kindly and simple men it has ever been my privilege to meet" (*International Studio* 79 [June 1924]: 228).

5. This anecdote is told by Helen M. Knowlton in *Art-Life of William Morris Hunt* (Boston, 1899), p. 7.

6. *Le merveilleux de cette exécution, outre la science du dessin et la beauté de la couleur, est une touche déliberée, libre, sans aucune fatigué, légère, et pourtant trés vigoureuse.* Theophile Thoré, "Salon de 1847," in *Salons de T. Thoré* (Paris, 1868), p. 431.

7. Couture explains his method in his *Méthode et entretiens d'atelier* (Paris, 1867); quotations in this text are from the English translation by S. E. Stewart,

Conversations on Art Methods (New York, 1879). For modern discussions of his method see: Albert Boime, *The Academy and French Painting in the Nineteenth Century* (London, 1971), especially pp. 65–78; Alain de Leiris, "Thomas Couture the Painter," in University of Maryland Art Gallery, *Thomas Couture: Paintings and Drawings in American Collections* (College Park, 1970), pp. 11–25; Marchal E. Landgren, "Thomas Couture the Teacher," in University of Maryland Art Gallery, *American Pupils of Thomas Couture* (College Park, 1970), pp. 9–19; and his "Thomas Couture, Painter and Teacher of Painters," *Antiques* 99 (June 1971): 877–81.

8. Royal Cortissoz, *John La Farge* (Boston, New York, 1911), p. 96.

9. Thoré, *Salons*, pp. 414–15.

10. All quotations pertaining to Newman's first visit to the Louvre were printed in "Museums of Art: Musée du Louvre," *Nashville Union and American*, December 12, 1872. Reynolds's first visit to the Vatican is reported in Cunningham's *Lives*, with which Newman was familiar; Reynolds was humiliated at not recognizing the work of Raphael on first sight.

11. The last four lines of Shelley's poem, *To* —, which begins, "One word [love] is too often profaned/For me to profane it."

12. Tupper (1810–1889) was an English poet who had given up the law to write verse; his *Proverbial Philosophy*, published in four series between 1839 and 1876, was a popular collection of moral statements in blank verse and went through many editions.

13. By the terms of his stepfather's will, Newman and his sister were to receive "the two lots in the town of Clarksville purchased from John H. Poston," in the event of the death of their mother (Montgomery County Records, Clerk's Office, Book J, p. 230). In addition to the two lots, Newman relinquished his interest in "the following negro property to wit one negro woman Amy aged about thirty and her child James aged about five years a negro girl named Gertrude aged about seven years and a negro woman Frances age about seventeen and her child James aged about one year" (Montgomery County Records, Register's Office, Deed Record Book 4, p. 302).

14. This story, together with the other facts related to Newman's 1854 sojourn in Paris, are recorded in a letter dated April 17, 1919, from Nestor Sanborn to Frederic Fairchild Sherman, now in the Frick Art Reference Library, New York. Mr. Barrett and the sum of money he lent Newman's mother are identified in the Montgomery County Deed Record Book 4.

15. Newman to Jefferson Davis, letter dated April 9, 1864. This letter and other letters quoted in this section, as well as facts pertaining to Newman's service with the Confederate army, are filed with his service record in Record Group 109, "Rebel Archives, War Department, Record Division," National Archives, Washington, D.C.

16. Sanborn's notes on Newman, *Brooklyn Museum Quarterly* 8 (October 1921): 157–61.

17. *Ibid.*, p. 158.

18. Montgomery County Records, Register's Office, Record Book 8, p. 531.

19. Newman to William W. Fergusson, letter dated December 7, 1872. Fergusson (1831–1922), a boyhood friend of Newman's, was a lawyer and educator, then living at Riddleton (near Carthage) outside Nashville, where he had founded the Blackgnat Academy. His letters are preserved in the Manuscript Section of

the Tennessee State Library and Archives, Nashville.

20. Nashville *Republican Banner*, September 25, 1872.

21. Newman to Fergusson, November 8, 1872.

22. Fergusson Papers, Tennessee State Library and Archives, Nashville.

23. The date of his mother's death is uncertain; on her tombstone, it has been read as both 1870 and 1879; court records, however, indicate that she died in 1873 (R. Lemmons, et al, vs J. B. Shearer, et al, Montgomery County Records, Chancery Court Clerk & Master's Office, Minutes, June Special Term, 1914, Book 25, p. 495).

24. Subsequent major mutations are the Armory Show of 1913, which can be seen in relation to the democratic spirit that sparked the Society of Independent Artists in 1917 and marked the federal patronage of art during the Great Depression, and the influx of European artists in America during the second World War, which unwittingly altered the democratic spirit by removing the voice of the artist from the affairs of his profession. Historians of American art have generally neglected the study of the artist with relationship to the standards of his profession, a neglect that some of the younger historians appear to be correcting.

25. Quoted in *Letters of Richard Watson Gilder*, ed. by his daughter Rosamond Gilder (Boston and New York, 1916), pp. 79–80.

26. *Scribner's Monthly* 10 (June 1875): 253.

27. Quoted, but not identified, in *Letters of Richard Watson Gilder*, p. 80.

28. [Clarence Cook] "About an American School of Art," *Scribner's Monthly* 10 (July 1875): 381.

29. William C. Brownell, "The Younger Painters of America," pt. 1, *Scribner's Monthly* 20 (May 1880): 2.

30. See Pauline King, *American Mural Painting* (Boston, 1902), for the story of the rise of mural painting in America.

31. Sanborn to Frederic Fairchild Sherman, letter dated April 17, 1919, in the Frick Art Reference Library, New York.

32. Brownell, "Young Painters," p. 2.

33. Newman to Mr. Bartlett, Boston, letter dated October 1, 1881, in the Boston Public Library, Manuscript Section.

34. The Hunt brought $600 and the Monginot, $200, according to an old record book, formerly in the possession of Doll and Richards.

35. Popular criticism of Newman's work over the years has almost invariably centered on the influence of Millet, Diaz, and Monticelli, but not on what distinguishes his work from theirs.

36. Sanborn to Sherman, April 17, 1919.

37. Samuel A. Chapin to the author, letter dated August 14, 1934. Marchal E. Landgren Papers.

38. *Ibid.* Newman became sixty in 1887; he appeared to be an old man to Chapin, who was then twenty-eight; Eaton was thirty-eight.

39. George S. Hellman, "Wyatt Eaton," *Art World*, December 1917, p. 204.

40. Sadakichi Hartmann, *A History of American Art* (Boston, 1901); rev. ed., 2 vols. (Boston, 1932), 1: 188.

41. From the records of M. Knoedler & Co., New York.

42. "The Newman Exhibition at Knoedler's," *The Critic*, no. 629, March 10, 1894.

43. *New York Tribune*, March 4, 1894.

44. *Boston Herald* (?), undated clipping, Museum of Fine Arts, Boston.

45. *Boston Sunday Herald*, April 1, 1894.

46. It is not known when and where French and Newman came to know one another, but labels on the stretchers of two Newman canvases owned by French indicate that he either submitted, or planned to submit, them to the 1896 exhibition of the Society of American Artists. One of the two canvases, *Mother and Child* (cat. no. 112), was lent by French to the 1899 exhibition. French was, of course, a friend of the Gilders and of many of Newman's artist friends.

47. Mrs. French to the author, letter dated August 20, 1934. Marchal E. Landgren Papers.

48. Daniel Chester French to Frederic Fairchild Sherman, letter dated April 25, 1919, in the Frick Art Reference Library, New York. The "shortcomings" were undoubtedly centered on Newman's willingness to be dependent upon others and his utter lack of financial responsibility.

49. *Ibid.*

50. Mrs. Alexander W. Drake to the author, letter dated December 1, 1934. Marchal E. Landgren Papers.

51. Sanborn to Sherman, April 17, 1919.

52. The New York and the Brooklyn directories list her at Bible House as early as 1884. In conversations with the author in 1934 and 1935, Mrs. Richard K. Maguire of Brooklyn, who was a pupil of Mrs. Sanborn's and who bought two Newmans at the Bible House sales (fig. 37 and cat. no. 68), mentioned that she often met Newman and Albert P. Ryder at the studio.

53. Patrick O'Connor, the son of the sculptor, to the author, letter dated February 10, 1973, written the day after a conversation with his mother. Marchal E. Landgren Papers.

54. Sanborn's notes on Newman, *Brooklyn Museum Quarterly*, p. 159.

55. Mrs. Frederick T. Van Beuren, letter to the author postmarked January 20, 1973; Mr. and Mrs. Van Beuren visited Newman and bought his paintings. There is an entry in the unpublished diary of Theodore Robinson, machine copy in the Frick Art Reference Library, New York, which indicates that on January 23, 1895, Newman had one of the new studios in Carnegie Hall, but found it "too noisy"; he apparently moved back to the Studio Building, for the American Art Annual of 1900, gives his address at 51 West Tenth Street, New York.

56. Sanborn to Sherman, April 17, 1919.

57. *Ibid.*

58. *Ibid.*

59. *A Good Story, Portrait of Robert Newman*, oil on canvas, 42 x 32½ inches, William T. Evans Collection, National Collection of Fine Arts, Washington.

60. Obituary, *New York Sun*, April 1, 1912.

61. Obituary, *New York Call*, April 1, 1912.

62. Sanborn to Sherman, April 17, 1919.

63. Obituary, *New York Herald*, April 1, 1912.

64. Sanborn to Sherman, April 17, 1919.

65. See Albert Boime, "Newman, Ryder, Couture and Hero-Worship in Art History," *American Art Journal* 3 (Fall 1971) : 5–22.

66. G. W. Sheldon, *American Painters*, enl. ed. (New York, 1881), p. 169.

67. Lloyd Goodrich, *Albert P. Ryder* (New York, 1959), p. 14.

68. From an interview with Ryder by Walter Pach ("On Albert P. Ryder," *Scribner's Magazine* 49 [January 1911] : 125–8), quoted in Goodrich, *Ryder*, p. 22.

69. *Ibid.*

70. The late Samuel A. Chapin, who had rooms adjoining those of Newman's, in a letter to the author dated August 14, 1934, places him there in the early 1880s. Marchal E. Landgren Papers.

71. Sadakichi Hartmann, *A History of American Art* 1 : 312.

72. The Newman-Ryder exhibition, held at M. Knoedler & Co., New York, in 1939, clearly revealed the difference in the capabilities of Newman and Ryder. In reviewing that exhibition ("A View of Two Native Romantics," *Art News*, November 11, 1939, pp. 9ff.), James W. Lane wrote, "Newman carries off all the honors in this comparison of work, because, while the ground against which his figures are set has no less murk than Ryder's, his figures, even when dimly shown, are drawn with more subtlety and with an exactitude in color values and shading which is astonishing."

73. The description and the attribution are taken from the catalog of the Stanford White sale, American Art Association, New York, April 11, 12, 1907, no. 100; such a subject could hardly be Early Venetian, and, if Venetian, would probably date to the sixteenth century.

74. Their marriage license is on file in the Rutherford County Court House, Murfreesboro; it was issued on December 24, 1896. Mrs. Newman's sister, Mrs. Mannie Todd Jackson of Murfreesboro, in a telephone conversation with the author, supplied the information on Mr. and Mrs. Newman.

75. Clarence Cook, *New York Tribune*, June 5, 1877.

76. Sanborn to Sherman, April 17, 1917.

77. The story of Sappho's rejection by Phaon was popular during the nineteenth century in romantic literature as a story of the solitude of genius; Franz Grillparzer, the Austrian author, dramatized the story in 1818, and his play was translated into English in 1858. Daudet's Sappho was written in 1884 and turned into an opera by Massenet in 1897; Clyde Fitch dramatized the story for the American stage.

78. *The Vicar of Wakefield* by Oliver Goldsmith is the story of a modern-day Job; the episode in which the vicar's daughters consult the fortune-teller immediately precedes the narration of the misfortunes that befall the vicar and his family.

79. Such notable personages of the seventeenth century as Mme. de Sévigné

and Charles Colbert found much pleasure in fairy tales, and Charles Perrault's renderings of them, *Histoire ou contes du temps passé*, published in 1697, were not intended for children. Gustave Doré illustrated an edition of Perrault's tales, about 1860, which Newman may have known, and *Grimm's Fairly Tales* were published between 1812 and 1815. A portrait of Emily Anderson as Red Ridinghood by Thomas Lawrence was widely known in this country through engravings by John Sartain (1852) and others, and E. Maurice Bloch in his *George Caleb Bingham, the Evolution of an Artist* (Berkeley and Los Angeles, 1967) notes that "at least thirteen paintings of [Red Ridinghood] appeared between 1838 and 1866 in the exhibitions of the National Academy of Design and the American Art-Union in New York and of the Pennsylvania Academy and the Artists Fund Society in Philadelphia (pp. 249–50)." The American sculptor William Wetmore Story, according to William H. Gerdts (*American Art Journal* 4 [November 1972] : 23) adapted the theme to sculpture.

80. Cf. Philippe Ariès, *Centuries of Childhood* (London, 1962), pp. 339–64.

81. Duncan Phillips, *A Collection in the Making* (New York, 1926), p. 38.

82. *New York Tribune*, March 4, 1894.

83. Margaret Breuning, "Ryder and Newman," *Magazine of Art* 32 (December 1939) : 714–16.

84. Heinrich Wölfflin, *Principles of Art History*, trans. M. D. Hottinger (New York, 1932), p. 226.

85. Reynolds's *Discourses* have been published in many editions; the quotation in this paragraph is from the Fourth Discourse, December 10, 1771.

86. George P. Mras, "Literary Sources of Delacroix's Conception of the Sketch and the Imagination," *Art Bulletin* 44 (June 1962) : 106.

87. René Huyghe, *Delacroix* (New York, 1963), p. 391.

88. Quoted in Klaus Berger, *Odilon Redon: Fantasy and Color* (New York, 1965), p. 112.

89. *Ibid.*

90. Quoted from *Soi-Même* in Maurice Serullaz, *The Impressionist Painters*, trans. W. J. Strahan (New York and Paris, 1960), p. 163.

91. Huyghe, *Delacroix*, pp. 390–98, gives a detailed account of Delacroix's practices.

92. Quoted in Huyghe, *Delacroix*, p. 383.

93. See Anita Brookner, "Baudelaire," in her *Genius of the Future* (London and New York, 1971), p. 78.

94. Bernard Berenson, *The Italian Painters of the Renaissance* (London, 1952), p. 199.

95. *Vasari's Lives of the Artists*, ed. and abr. Betty Burroughs (New York, 1946), p. 247.

96. Jean Seznec and Jean Adhémar, *Diderot Salons*, 4 vols. (Oxford, 1957–67), 1: 222.

97. Cézanne advised Emile Bernard to "treat nature by the cylinder, the sphere, the cone, everything in proper perspective so that each side of an object or a plane is directed toward a central point." Quoted in Robert Goldwater, ed., *Artists on Art* (New York, 1945), p. 363.

98. Albert Gleizes and Jean Metzinger, *Cubism* (London, 1913), p. 27. Bernhard Riemann (1822–1866), professor of mathematics at the University of Göttingen, laid the foundations of non-Euclidean geometries in his inaugural address at the university in 1851; an English translation of that address, "On the Hypotheses which Lie at the Bases of Geometry," was published in *Nature*, May 1, 1873. Mathematicians will recognize a similarity between Cézanne's planes and the elliptical points of Riemannian geometry, with the plane of the canvas serving as the tangent plane. Mathematical studies leading to Riemann's work began at the École Polytechnique, Paris, particularly under Gaspard Monge (1746–1818) and his pupil Victor Poncelet (1788–1867), who studied the persistence of certain geometrical properties of figures, when those figures were subjected to deformation, as when the artist portrays three-dimensional objects on a two-dimensional surface. Richard Courant and Herbert Robbins in *What is Mathematics?* [New York and London, 1941], p. 167, point out that such study "was forced upon mathematicians long ago by the problems of perspective, which were studied by such artists as Leonardo da Vinci and Albrecht Dürer." The Cubists, in referring to the theorems of Riemann, were in effect simply referring to problems that originated with the artist.

99. Berenson, in his studies of Renaissance art, equated the perception of form with such "tactile values . . . as volume, bulk, inner substance, and texture," *Italian Painters of the Renaissance*, pp. 199–200.

100. Lewis Mumford, *The Brown Decades* (New York, 1955), p. 50.

101. *New York Post*, March 3, 1894.

102. Quoted from the introduction by William H. Fox to Brooklyn Museum, *Works of American Painters 1860–1885* (Brooklyn, N.Y., 1917).

103. Phillips, *Collection in the Making*, p. 38.

Chronology

1827 Born, November 10, at Richmond, Virginia, the second and last child, and only son, of Robert L. and Sarah J. (Matthews) Newman; his sister Eliza Jane was born at Richmond, August 26, 1823.
His father dies when Newman is a young child, and his mother moves to nearby Luisa Court House, Virginia.

1832 His mother remarries, to Joseph Winston.

1839 Moves with the family to Clarksville, Tennessee.

1844 His stepfather dies.

1846 Writes to Asher B. Durand, asking to be taken on as a pupil.

1849 Exhibits *Music on the Shop-Board* with the American Art-Union, New York.

1850 Takes his first trip abroad and enters the studio of Thomas Couture, Paris; remains with Couture for about five months before returning to Clarksville.

1854 Takes his second trip abroad; shares an apartment with Nathaniel Greene, author and editor of Boston, on the Chaussée d'Antin, Paris; is introduced to Barbizon and J. F. Millet by William Morris Hunt; returns to Clarksville.

1858 Inserts notices in Clarksville newspapers that he will open a studio in the spring in his home to advanced students and that he will accept commissions for full-length portraits.

1860 His mother enters into a third marriage, to John L. Swainey of Sumner County, Tennessee, but apparently continues to live at Clarksville; the outcome of the marriage is unknown; at the time of her death, she had resumed the name Sarah J. Winston, and her grave is so marked.

1861–1864 Elected a lieutenant of artillery in the Confederate army, but resigns over a disagreement with his commanding officer; is conscripted at Nashville, April 1864, and assigned to Company G, 15th Virginia Regiment, Richmond, Virginia.

1865	On April 18, after the fall of Richmond, receives a pass to the North with destination given as New York; is back at Clarksville by August 15.
1865–1871	Probably in New York.
1872–1873	Spends the winter months at Nashville, Tennessee, where he advertises as a portrait painter and a teacher of drawing and painting; attempts to found an Academy of Fine Arts with George Dury (1817–1894), a portrait painter; his mother dies in 1873.
1873–1879	In New York, is employed for a short time by Francis Lathrop in the design of stained glass.
1880	Lives at 64 Washington Square South, New York.
1882	Takes his third trip abroad, spending time at Barbizon; returns to New York.
1882–1892	Lives during this period, or part of it, with Wyatt Eaton at the Benedict Chambers, 80 Washington Square East, New York; in 1886, exhibits a *Little Red Ridinghood* at the fifth autumn exhibition of the National Academy of Design, New York.
1894	The only exhibition of his work during his lifetime is held at M. Knoedler & Company, 170 Fifth Avenue, New York, March 1–15; more than half of the exhibition is shown at the Museum of Fine Arts, Boston, March 27–April 17; lives at 51 West Tenth Street, New York.
1895	Moves to one of the new studios in Carnegie Hall, New York, but dissatisfied, returns to 51 West Tenth Street.
1899	Exhibits *Mother and Child* (cat. no. 112) in twenty-first exhibition of the Society of American Artists, New York, 1899.
1900	Moves to 250 West Fourteenth Street, New York; *Christ Stilling the Tempest* (fig. 33) is shown in the fine arts exhibit of the United States, Paris International Exposition, 1900.
1906–1908	Lives at 119 East Twenty-third Street, New York.
1908	With proceeds of sale of his works at Mrs. Sanborn's studio, takes a fourth trip abroad, spending some time at Andrew O'Connor's residence at Clamart, near Paris; returns to New York.
1909	Another studio sale at Mrs. Sanborn's enables him to take his fifth and last trip abroad.
1910–1912	Lives at 243 President Street, Brooklyn.
1912	Moves to 206 East Eigtheenth Street, New York, on March

30; the following day, is found dead of asphyxiation by gas escaping from a heater in his room.

1914 The Brooklyn Museum becomes the first museum to acquire one of his works, *Madonna and Child* (fig. 72), gift of A. Augustus Healy.

1916 Frederic Fairchild Sherman publishes the first critical estimate of his work in *Art in America*, April issue.

1918 The Brooklyn Museum purchases seven of his canvases from Nestor Sanborn.

1921 Mrs. Wallace Sawyer presents *Saint John the Baptist* (fig. 73) and *The Fortune Teller* (fig. 74) to the Metropolitan Museum of Art; Nestor Sanborn contributes notes on his life and a critique of his work to the *Brooklyn Museum Quarterly*, October issue.

1924 Frank K. M. Rehn, New York, mounts an exhibition of thirty-three of his works, from which Duncan Phillips purchases *The Letter* (fig. 76) and *The Skylark* (fig. 77), both now in the Phillips Collection, Washington, D.C., and the Newark Museum acquires *The Good Samaritan* (fig. 75).

1935 The Whitney Museum of American Art, New York, mounts an exhibition of fifty-one paintings and six drawings.

1939 M. Knoedler & Company, New York, mounts a joint exhibition of his work and the work of Albert Pinkham Ryder.

1942 The Virginia Museum of Fine Arts, Richmond, mounts a memorial exhibition of thirty-seven paintings and seven drawings.

1961 The Graham Gallery, New York, exhibits the thirty-odd canvases collected by the late Joseph Katz of Baltimore.

Catalog of Known Works

The works of Robert Loftin Newman are widely scattered, and many of them have undergone several changes of ownership. Paintings that were known thirty of forty years ago have somehow disappeared, often because their owners have died, leaving no heirs, or heirs that have proved difficult or impossible to trace. Very few of Newman's works appear in exhibitions or in the marketplace, which, of course, adds to the difficulty of locating them. Forty years ago, when this catalog was begun, it was still possible to trace members of the families that had lent works to the Newman exhibition held at Knoedler's in 1894. That possibility made the initial cataloging of his works a feasible venture.

All of Newman's known works, whether or not their present locations are known, are listed here, if there is sufficient information to identify them. They are illustrated, whenever possible, by photographs collected over the years. Every effort has been made to restore their original titles, which also have often undergone many changes.

Height precedes width in the dimensions of the works, which are given first in inches and then in centimeters (in parentheses). In recording the provenance of the works, dates enclosed in parentheses, e.g., (1894), indicate that they were known to be in the possession of the person named by that time; dates not so enclosed indicate the year of their acquisition by the person named.

The following abbreviations are used in the references:

Boston 1894 Boston. Museum of Fine Arts. *Paintings by Robert Loftin Newman*; exhibition, March 27–April 17, 1894.

Graham 1961 Graham Gallery, New York. *Robert Loftin Newman 1827–1912*; exhibition, September 20–October 21, 1961.

Knoedler 1894 M. Knoedler & Co., New York. *Loan Collection of Paintings by Mr. R. L. Newman*; exhibition, March 1–15, 1894.

Knoedler 1939 M. Knoedler & Co., New York. *Two American Romantics of the Nineteenth Century: Robert Loftin Newman, Albert Pinkham Ryder*; exhibition, November 13–December 2, 1939.

Rehn 1924 Frank K. M. Rehn Galleries, New York. *Loan Collection of Paintings by Robert Loftin Newman*; exhibition, April 14–May 5, 1924.

Virginia 1942 Virginia Museum of Fine Arts, Richmond. *A Memorial Exhibition of the Work of Robert Loftin Newman*, January 26–February 27, 1942.

Whitney 1935 Whitney Museum of American Art, New York. *Paintings by Robert Loftin Newman*; exhibition, January 15–February 8, 1935.

Religious Subjects

1 ADAM AND EVE *figure 78*
oil on canvas, 10 x 6 (25.4 x 15.2)
Mrs. George W. Remaily, Hammondsport, New York

Provenance: Alexander W. Drake, New York, purchased from the artist and passed on, after the death of his widow, to his granddaughter, the present owner.

References: Whitney 1935, no. 37; F. F. Sherman, "Robert Loftin Newman," *Art in America* 27 (April 1939): 75; Knoedler 1939, no. 35; *Art Digest,* November 15, 1939, illus. p. 13; Virginia 1942, no. 25, pl. 15.

2 ADORATION
oil on canvas, 8⅞ x 12 (22.5 x 30.5)
Signed: R L Newman, lower right
The Brooklyn Museum, Brooklyn, New York (18.27.19)

Provenance: Nestor Sanborn, Brooklyn, New York, probably purchased from the artist, sold to the Brooklyn Museum, 1918.

References: Brooklyn Museum, *Works by American Painters 1860-1885,* exhibition, November 1-29, 1917, no. 57, under title *Mother and Child with Two Children Presenting a Lily;* Whitney 1935, no. 49; Knoedler 1939, no. 21; Virginia 1942, no. 21; *The Hand and the Spirit,* exhibition sponsored by the Graduate Theological Union, Berkeley, the University Art Museum, Berkeley, and the National Collection of Fine Arts, Washington, D. C. (Berkeley, 1972), no. 96.

Related Works: The Flight into Egypt, cat. no. 16; fig. 69, cat. no. 17.

3 ADORATION

oil on canvas, 14 x 12 (35.5 x 30.5)
Signed: R L Newman, lower right
Present location unknown

The title given here is traditional; a more correct title would be *Madonna with Saint Joseph and Saint John.*

Provenance: Johann Bertelson; Milch Galleries, New York; Babcock Galleries, New York (1945); Mrs. Huttleston Rogers, Taos, New Mexico, 1945; Rogers sale, Parke-Bernet Galleries, New York, 2d session, December 3, 1954, no. 226, to Babcock Galleries, New York; Ferargil Galleries, New York, 1955.

References: American-British Art Center, New York, *Other Worlds,* exhibition, October 8–27, 1945, no. 20.

4 AT PRAYER

oil on canvas, 14¼ x 10¼ (36.2 x 26)
Private collection, Fairfield, Connecticut

Provenance: Frank H. Scott, New York (1894), passed on to present owner.

References: Knoedler 1894, no. 79; Boston 1894, no. 63.

5 CHRIST AND THE APOSTLES *figure 9*

oil on canvas, 20 x 30 (50.8 x 76.2)
Mr. and Mrs. Cornelius Vanderbilt Whitney, New York

The painting now hangs in a church in Trujillo, Spain.

Provenance: Francis Lathrop, New York (1894); Lathrop sale, Anderson Art Galleries, New York, 1st session, April 4, 1911, no. 33; Hinsberg et al sale, Anderson Galleries, New York, December 16–17, 1912, no. 274; Huber Clark et al sale, S. T. Freeman & Co., Philadelphia, December 14, 1925, no. 35, to John F. Braun, Philadelphia; Whitney Museum of American Art, New York, 1935, sold to the present owners through M. Knoedler & Co., New York, 1950.

References: Knoedler 1894, no. 70; Whitney 1935, no. 51, illus. p. 19, under title *Christ and His Disciples;* F. F. Sherman, "Robert Loftin Newman," *Art in America* 27 (April 1939): 75; Knoedler 1939, no. 27, under title *Christ and His Disciples;* Carnegie Institute, Pittsburgh, Department of Fine Arts, *Survey of American Painting,* exhibition, October 24–December 15, 1940, no. 153, under title *Christ and His Disciples;* Virginia 1942, no. 12, pl. 4, under title *Christ and His Disciples.*

6 CHRIST AND THE APOSTLES
oil on canvas, 10 x 14 (25.4 x 35.6)
Present location unknown

Provenance: Francis Lathrop, New York, purchased from the artist; Lathrop sale, Anderson Art Galleries, New York, 2d session, April 5, 1911, no. 104.

7 CHRIST AND THE FIGURE BY THE WAYSIDE, A SKETCH 1900
oil on canvas, 16 x 13 (40.6 x 33)
Signed and dated 1900
Present location unknown

Provenance: Victor G. Fischer Art Co., Washington, D.C.; Fischer Art Co. sale, Anderson Galleries, New York, February 19, 1912, no. 124.

8 CHRIST AND THE MAGDALEN *figure 38*
oil on canvas, 10⅛ x 14⅛ (25.7 x 35.9)
Victor D. Spark, New York, and Graham Gallery, New York

Provenance: Macbeth Gallery, New York (1909); George S. Hellman, New York (1919); sale no. 1446, Anderson Galleries, New York, November 21, 1919, no. 38, to Nestor Sanborn, Brooklyn, New York; Arthur Egner, South Orange, New Jersey, 1924; Egner sale, Parke-Bernet Galleries, New York, May 4, 1945, no. 19, illus., under title *Noli me tangere,* to Babcock Galleries, New York; Joseph Katz, Baltimore, 1945.

References: Rehn 1924, no. 14; Virginia 1942, no. 35, under title *Christ Appearing to Mary;* Graham 1961, no. 30, also under title *Christ Appearing to Mary.*

Related Works: Rabboni, fig. 37, cat. no. 39.

9 CHRIST LIFTING SAINT PETER FROM THE WAVES *figure 31*
oil on canvas, 12¼ x 14¾ (31.1 x 37.5)
Signed: R L Newman, lower left
Portland Art Museum, Portland, Oregon. Gift of Mrs. William M. Ladd, 1931, in memory of her husband

Provenance: Probably the work of the same title owned by E. K. Rossiter, New York (1894); purchased by Daniel Cottier & Co., New York, 1894, and sold to William M. Ladd, Portland, Oregon.

References: Knoedler 1894, no. 76?; Boston 1894, no. 61?; *The Hand and the Spirit,* exhibition sponsored by the Graduate Theological Union, Berkeley, the University Art Museum, Berkeley, and the National Collection of Fine Arts, Washington, D.C. (Berkeley, 1972), no. 94, under title *Christ and Peter on the Sea of Galilee.*

Related Works: Christ Saving Peter, cat. no. 10.

10 CHRIST SAVING PETER
oil on canvas, 16 x 20 (40.6 x 50.8)
Signed: R L Newman, lower left
The Brooklyn Museum, Brooklyn, New York (18.29)

Provenance: Nestor Sanborn, Brooklyn, N.Y. (1917), probably purchased from the artist; Brooklyn Museum, 1918.

References: Brooklyn Museum, *Works by American Painters 1860–1885,* exhibition, November 1–29, 1917, no. 55; Whitney 1935, no. 38; F. F. Sherman, "Robert Loftin Newman," *Art in America* 27 (April 1939): 75; Virginia 1942, no. 20; Albert Boime, "Newman, Ryder, Couture," *American Art Journal* 3 (Fall 1971): fig. 4.

Related Works: Christ Lifting Saint Peter from the Waves, fig. 31, cat. no. 9.

11 CHRIST STILLING THE TEMPEST *figure 33*

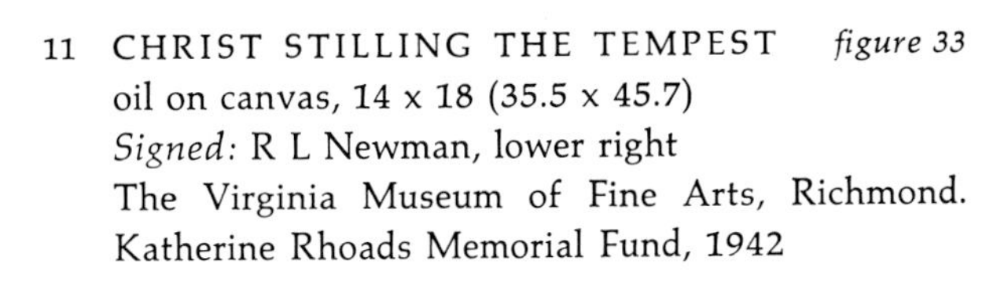

oil on canvas, 14 x 18 (35.5 x 45.7)
Signed: R L Newman, lower right
The Virginia Museum of Fine Arts, Richmond. Katherine Rhoads Memorial Fund, 1942

Provenance: William T. Evans, New York (1898); Evans sale, American Art Association, New York, 3d evening session, February 2, 1900, no. 192, to Edward D. Page; Elliot Daingerfield (1922); Frank K. M. Rehn, New York, 1924; offered at sale, American Art Association, New York, April 8–11, 1931, no. 108, withdrawn?; Mrs. Nettie S. Horch, New York (1935).

References: Paris Exposition of 1900, Fine Arts Exhibit of the United States (Boston, 1900), no. 240; Rehn 1924, no. 4; *Arts* 5 (May 1924): Illus. p. 291; Whitney 1935, no. 24; Knoedler 1939, no. 38; Virginia 1942, no. 26, pl. 16; Albert Boime, "Newman, Ryder, Couture," *American Art Journal* 3 (Fall 1971): fig. 3; W. H. Truettner, "William T. Evans," *American Art Journal* 3 (Fall 1971): 77.

12 CHRIST WALKING ON THE WATER
oil on canvas, 10 x 16 (25.5 x 40.7)
Signed: R L Newman, lower left
The Brooklyn Museum, Brooklyn, New York. Gift of Mrs. Frederic B. Pratt, 1925 (25.62)

Provenance: Macbeth Gallery, New York, to Mrs. Pratt, 1896.

13 THE ENTOMBMENT *figure 8*
oil on canvas, 6 x 8 (15.2 x 20.3)
Signed: R L Newman, lower right
Mrs. William Penn Cresson, Stockbridge, Massachusetts

Newman made this sketch, probably from memory, after Titian's *Entombment* in the Louvre.

Provenance: Daniel Chester French, New York (1898), purchased from the artist and passed on to his daughter, the present owner.

14 THE FINDING OF MOSES 1899 *figure 13*
oil on canvas, 10 x 16 (25.4 x 40.6)
Signed: R L Newman 1899, lower right
Mr. and Mrs. William J. Poplack, Birmingham, Michigan

Provenance: Joint purchase of James Graham and Victor D. Spark, New York, at auction near Albany, New

York, 1951; Joseph Katz, Baltimore; Victor D. Spark and Graham Gallery, New York (1961).

References: Graham 1961, no. 25.

15 THE FLIGHT INTO EGYPT
oil on canvas, 9 x 11¼ (22.9 x 28.6)
Graham Gallery, New York

References: Probably Rehn 1924, no. 18.

16 THE FLIGHT INTO EGYPT
oil on canvas, 12¼ x 18 (31.1 x 45.7)
Signed: R L Newman, lower left
Present location unknown

Mary, in dark blue draperies over crimson, is seated holding the Child, while Joseph, in a dull purplish robe, leads the ass toward the light of the morning sky. An angel, at left, has robes and wings of pink and white.

Provenance: Dowdeswell & Dowdeswell and T. J. Blakeslee sale, American Art Association, New York, April 7, 1904, no. 74b (not in catalog); J. M. Lichtenauer sale, American Art Association, New York, February 27–28, 1913, no. 42, to Holland Art Galleries, New York; sold to John F. Braun, Philadelphia, by G. Castano, Boston.

References: Whitney 1935, no. 2.

Related Works: Adoration, cat. no. 2; *The Flight into Egypt,* fig. 69, cat. no. 17.

17 THE FLIGHT INTO EGYPT *figure 69*
oil on canvas, 14 x 18 (35.6 x 45.7)
Signed: R L Newman, lower left
The Virginia Museum of Fine Arts, Richmond

Provenance: Administrator's sale, estate of the artist, Fifth Avenue Art Galleries, New York, June 6, 1912, no. 6; Albert Schneider; Babcock Galleries, New York, 1946; Joseph Katz, Baltimore (1954).

References: Graham 1961, no. 8, under title *Madonna and Child and Angels;* Albert Boime, "Newman, Ryder, Couture," *American Art Journal,* 3 (Fall 1971): fig. 9.

Related Works: Adoration, cat. no. 2; *The Flight into Egypt,* cat. no. 16.

18 THE FLIGHT INTO EGYPT
oil on canvas, 20 x 30 (50.8 x 76.2)
Signed: R L Newman, lower left
Present location unknown

Provenance: Purchased by Miss Palmie at Mrs. Sanborn's studio sale, 1909; E. C. Babcock, New York, 1926; Hon. John G. Winant, Concord, New Hampshire, 1928.

References: F. F. Sherman, "Robert Loftin Newman," *Art in America* 27 (April 1939): 75.

19 THE GOOD SAMARITAN *figure 28*
oil on canvas, 9¼ x 11⅛ (23.5 x 28.3)
Signed: R L Newman, lower right
Victor D. Spark, New York, and Graham Gallery, New York

Provenance: Robert Underwood Johnson, New York (1894), passed on to his daughter Mrs. Frank H. Holden, 1937; Joseph Katz, Baltimore.

References: Knoedler 1894, no. 50; Boston 1894, no. 39; Rehn 1924, no. 24; Whitney 1935, no. 29; F. F. Sherman, "Robert Loftin Newman," *Art in America* 27 (April 1939): 75; Virginia 1942, no. 4; Graham 1961, no. 29.

20 THE GOOD SAMARITAN 1886 *figure 75*
oil on canvas, 9 x 11 (22.9 x 28)
Signed: R L Newman 1886, lower left
The Newark Museum, Newark, New Jersey. Gift of Mrs. Felix Fuld

Provenance: John Gellatly, New York (1894), probably purchased from the artist; Frank K. M. Rehn Gallery, New York, 1919; Newark Museum, 1924.

References: Knoedler 1894, no. 27; Boston 1894, no. 21; Rehn 1924, no. 15 or 20; *Arts* 5 (May 1924): illus. p. 292; *International Studio* 79 (June 1924): illus. p. 228; Whitney 1935, no. 13; Virginia 1942, no. 37; Newark Museum, *A Museum in Action* (Newark, New Jersey, 1944), no. 48; *The Hand and the Spirit,* exhibition sponsored by the Graduate Theological Union, Berkeley, the University Art Museum, Berkeley, and the National Collection of Fine Arts, Washington, D.C. (Berkeley, 1972), no. 97, illus.

Related Works: The Good Samaritan, fig. 70, cat. no. 21.

21 THE GOOD SAMARITAN 1886 *figure 70*
oil on canvas, 10 x 14 (25.4 x 35.5)
Signed: R L Newman 1886, lower right
Mrs. Hugh C. Thompson, Tucson, Arizona

Provenance: Clarence Clough Buel, New York (1894), purchased from the artist and passed on, after the death of his widow, to his daughter, the present owner.

References: Knoedler 1894, no. 11; Whitney 1935, no. 52; M. E. Landgren, "Robert Loftin Newman," *American Magazine of Art* 28 (March 1935): illus. p. 140; Knoedler 1939, no. 33; J. W. Lane, "A View of Two Native Romantics," *Art News* 38 (November 11, 1939): illus. p. 9; *Parnassus* 11 (November 1939): illus. p. 38; Virginia 1942, no. 22, pl. 14; University of Maryland Art Gallery, *American Pupils of Thomas Couture*, exhibition, March 19–April 26, 1970, no. 34, illus.

Related Works: The Good Samaritan, fig. 75, cat. no. 20.

22 THE GOOD SAMARITAN 1898
oil on canvas, 19 x 17 (48.2 x 43.2)
Signed: R L Newman 1898, lower left
Mr. and Mrs. Paul Rothstein, Yonkers, New York

Provenance: L. Ettlinger (1917); sale, American Art Association, New York, March 16, 1917, no. 36, to M. S. Allen; probably the work of the same title owned by Mrs. Wallace Sawyer, Asbury Park, New Jersey in 1924; sale, Alfred Cooper, auctioneers, Yonkers, New York, summer 1972, to the present owner.

References: Rehn 1924, no. 15 or 20?

23 HAGAR *figure 30*
oil on canvas, 14 x 18 (35.5 x 45.7)
Signed: R L Newman, lower left
The Metropolitan Museum of Art, New York. Gift of Mrs. Wallace Sawyer, 1925

Provenance: Mrs. Wallace Sawyer, Asbury Park, New Jersey (1924).

References: Rehn 1924, no. 26, under title *Hagar in the Wilderness*; New York, Metropolitan Museum of Art, *Catalogue of Paintings*, by Bryson Burroughs, 9th ed. (New York, 1931), p. 263.

24 HAGAR AND ISHMAEL
oil on canvas, 12¼ x 16¼ (31.1 x 41.3)
Signed
Present location unknown

Provenance: Sir William C. Van Horne, Montreal (1894), probably purchased from the artist; passed on to his daughter Miss Adaline Van Horne (1934).

References: Knoedler 1894, no. 83; Boston 1894, no. 66; F. F. Sherman, "Robert Loftin Newman," *Art in America* 27 (April 1939): 75.

25 THE HOLY FAMILY *figure 18*
oil on canvas, 24 x 14 (61 x 35.5)
Signed: R L Newman, lower right
Mr. and Mrs. I. David Orr, New York

Provenance: Victor Harris, New York, probably purchased from the artist after 1894; Mrs. Victor Harris sale, Parke-Bernet Galleries, New York, 3d session, May 8, 1943, no. 607, to Babcock Galleries, New York; H. B. Harris, 1946; Babcock Galleries, New York, 1954, to present owners, 1959.

References: Probably the same as Knoedler 1894, no. 104, lent by the artist; Whitney 1935, no. 45; F. F. Sherman, "Robert Loftin Newman," *Art in America* 27 (April 1939): 75.

Related Works: Girl and Two Children, fig. 58, cat. no. 73; *Madonna and Child,* cat. no. 180. Three works under this title were lent to the exhibitions at New York and Boston in 1894; one was lent by Theron J. Blakeslee, New York; another by D. W. C. Morrell; and the third by the artist.

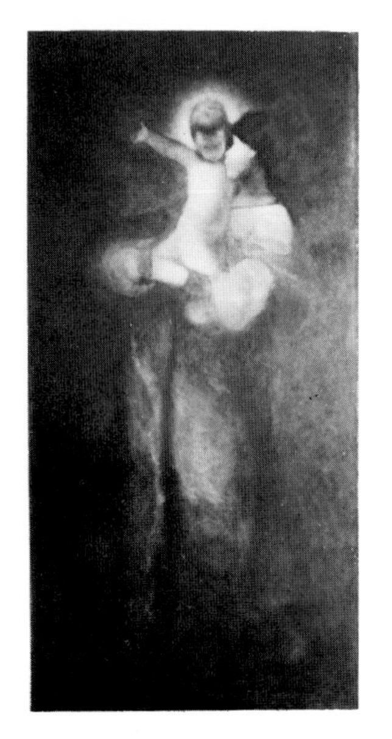

26 MADONNA AND CHILD
oil on canvas, 43½ x 22½ (110.5 x 57.2)
Signed: R L Newman, lower left
Catholic Library and Information Center of the Archdiocese of Hartford, Connecticut

Provenance: Theron J. Blakeslee, New York (1894); R. B. Angus, Montreal, 1894; Theron J. Blakeslee, New York (1900); Blakeslee sale, American Art Association, New York, 2d evening sale, March 10, 1900, no. 87, to Charles F. Sprague; Frank Gair Macomber, Boston (1936); Macomber sale, American Art Association, Anderson Galleries, New York, 3d session, December 12, 1936, no. 657, to Babcock Galleries, New York;

Rev. Andrew John Kelly, Hartford, Connecticut (1943), bequeathed to the present owners.

References: Knoedler 1894, no. 7; Boston 1894, no. 6; F. F. Sherman, "Robert Loftin Newman," *Art in America* 27 (April 1939): 75, illus. p. 100; Knoedler 1939, no. 30; Virginia 1942, no. 6.

27 MADONNA AND CHILD 1897 *figure 72*
oil on canvas, 23½ x 13½ (59.7 x 34.3)
Signed: R L Newman 1897, lower left
The Brooklyn Museum, Brooklyn, New York. Gift of A. Augustus Healy, 1914 (14.547).

Provenance: Probably the same work as that owned by Pincus Chock and sold at the Chock sale, American Art Association, New York, March 9–11, 1898, no. 43.

References: Brooklyn Museum, *Works of American Painters 1860–1885*, exhibition, November 1–29, 1917, no. 53, illus.; Nestor Sanborn, "Robert Loftin Newman, Colorist," *Brooklyn Museum Quarterly* 8 (October 1921): illus. p. 156; Tennessee Fine Arts Center, Nashville, *Tennessee Painting: The Past*, exhibition, May 22–July 31, 1960, no. 37.

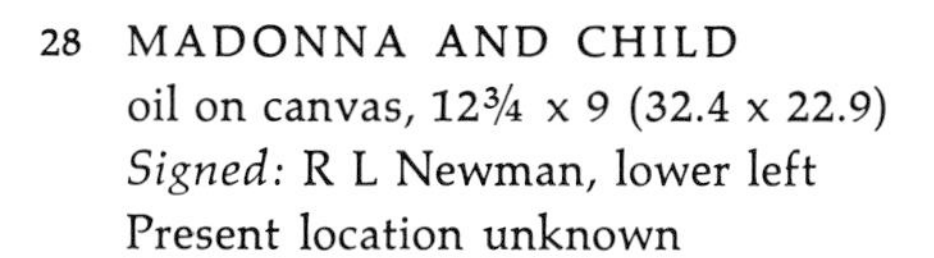

28 MADONNA AND CHILD
oil on canvas, 12¾ x 9 (32.4 x 22.9)
Signed: R L Newman, lower left
Present location unknown

Provenance: Robert Underwood Johnson, New York (1894); William T. Evans, New York, 1894; Evans sale, American Art Association, New York, 1st evening sale, January 31, 1900, no. 25, to R. H. Austin; William T. Evans (1902); Evans sale, American Art Association, New York, 3d evening sale, April 1, 1913, no. 148, to Prof. Herschel C. Parker, Brooklyn, New York; Macbeth Gallery, New York, 1924; Mrs. Frederic S. Lee, New York, 1929.

References: Knoedler 1894, no. 49; Boston 1894, no. 40; Rehn 1924, no. 17; Whitney 1935, no. 28; Knoedler 1939, no. 24; W. H. Truettner, "William T. Evans," *American Art Journal* 3 (Fall 1971): 77.

29 MADONNA AND CHILD *figure 3*
oil on canvas, 18 x 14 (45.7 x 35.5)
Signed: R L Newman, lower right
Mrs. Walter Sharp, Brentwood, Tennessee

Provenance: Mrs. D. P. Kimball, Boston (1894); Babcock Galleries, New York (1948); Walter Sharp, Nashville, Tennessee.

References: Knoedler 1894, no. 52; Boston 1894, no. 42.

30 MADONNA AND CHILD 1897 *figure 19*
oil on canvas, 20 x 16 (50.8 x 40.6)
Signed: R L Newman 1897, lower left
Private collection, Wilmington, Delaware

Provenance: Mrs. Alma Quint, purchased from the artist by her father; Milch Galleries, New York; Babcock Galleries, New York (1952); Joseph Katz, Baltimore (1954); Victor D. Spark and Graham Gallery, New York (1961).

References: Graham 1961, no. 17.

Related Works: Pincus Chock of New York owned two versions of the *Madonna and Child* in the same dimensions as this one; they were sold at the Chock sale, American Art Association, New York, March 9–11, 1898, nos. 145, 257.

31 MADONNA AND CHILD
oil on canvas, 9 x 7 (22.9 x 17.8)
Mr. and Mrs. Edwin Arthur Hill, Jr., New York

Provenance: Helena de Kay Gilder, New York (1894), probably purchased from the artist; New York art market, to the present owner, 1958.

References: Knoedler 1894, no. 40.

32 MADONNA AND CHILD *figure 20*

oil on canvas, 21¾ x 15¾ (55.2 x 40)
Signed: R L Newman, lower left
Tennessee Fine Arts Center Collection, Nashville

Provenance: Mrs. S. D. Warren (1894); Victor D. Spark, New York (1956).

References: Boston 1894, no. 85; University of Maryland Art Gallery, *American Pupils of Thomas Couture,* exhibition, March 19–April 26, 1970, no. 35, illus. p. 57; T. B. Brumbaugh, "Letters of Robert Loftin Newman," *Tennessee Historical Quarterly* 32 (Summer 1973): cover illus.

33 MADONNA AND CHILD

oil on canvas, 16 x 12 (40.7 x 30.5)
Signed: R L Newman, lower right
Scripps College, Claremont, California. Gift of Mrs. Young, 1946

Provenance: A. E. Rueff, New York; Klauder et al sale, S. T. Freeman & Co., Philadelphia, March 8–9, 1926, no. 157.

34 MADONNA AND CHILD 1909

oil on canvas, 10 x 6 (25.4 x 15.3)
Signed: R L Newman 1909, lower left
Present location unknown

Provenance: Johann Bertelson; Milch Galleries, New York; Babcock Galleries, New York (1950); the late Clare Hoffman, Perrysburg, Ohio, 1953.

35 THE MAGDALEN 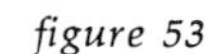 *figure 53*

oil on canvas, 11 x 9 (28 x 22.9)
Signed: R L Newman, lower right
Present location unknown

Provenance: Sir William C. Van Horne, Montreal (1894), purchased from the artist and passed on to his daughter Miss Adaline Van Horne (1934).

References: Knoedler 1894, no. 86; Boston 1894, no. 60; F. F. Sherman, "Robert Loftin Newman," *Art in America* 4 (April 1916): illus. facing p. 178; F. F. Sherman, *Landscape and Figure Painters of America* (New York, 1917), illus. facing p. 18.

36 MOTHER AND SON

oil on canvas, 12 x 8¾ (30.5 x 22.2)
Signed: R L Newman, lower left
Georgia Museum of Art, The University of Georgia, Athens. Gift of Alfred H. Holbrook, 1945

Provenance: John F. Braun, Philadelphia; Babcock Galleries, New York; Alfred H. Holbrook, Athens, Georgia.

37 THE NATIVITY

oil on canvas, 14 x 18 (35.5 x 45.7)
Signed: R L Newman, lower right
Present location unknown

Provenance: Ehrich-Newhouse Galleries, New York (1935); Pell et al sale, Parke-Bernet Galleries, New York, April 18, 1940, no. 41, to the late William T. Cresmer, Chicago.

References: Virginia 1942, no. 31.

38 THE PRODIGAL SON *figure 6*

oil on canvas, 14 x 16 (35.5 x 40.6)
Private collection, Washington, D.C.

Provenance: Francis Lathrop, New York (1894), purchased from the artist; Mrs. James Francis Brown, New York (1935); Telfair Academy of Arts and Sciences, Savannah, Georgia, 1944; present owner, 1972.

References: Knoedler 1894, no. 63; Boston 1894, no. 51; Virginia 1942, no. 27, pl. 13.

39 RABBONI *figure 37*

oil on canvas, 16 x 20 (40.6 x 50.8)
Signed: R L Newman, lower right
Present location unknown

Provenance: Mrs. Richard K. Maguire, Brooklyn, New York, purchased from the artist at Mrs. Sanborn's studio and passed on to her son Richard K. Maguire.

References: Whitney 1935, no. 20; F. F. Sherman, "Robert Loftin Newman," *Art in America* 27 (April 1939): 75.

Related Works: Christ and the Magdalen, fig. 38; cat. no. 8.

40 SAINT JOHN THE BAPTIST *figure 73*

oil on canvas, 10⅛ x 12⅛ (25.7 x 30.8)
The Metropolitan Museum of Art, New York. Gift of Mrs. Wallace Sawyer, 1921

Provenance: Mrs. Wallace Sawyer, Asbury Park, New Jersey, probably purchased from the artist.

References: New York, Metropolitan Museum of Art, *Catalogue of Paintings,* by Bryson Burroughs, 9th ed. (New York, 1931), p. 263; Whitney 1935, no. 42; M. E. Landgren, "Robert Loftin Newman," *American Magazine of Art* 28 (March 1935): illus. p. 136; F. F. Sherman, "Robert Loftin Newman," *Art in America* 27 (April 1939): 75; Virginia 1942, no. 14, pl. 6.

41 SALOME DANCING

oil on canvas, 20 x 15 (50.8 x 38.1)
Signed: R L Newman, lower left
Dr. William Arkwright Doppler, Florham Park, New Jersey

Newman undoubtedly took this subject from among the several depictions of Salome by Gustave Moreau, attracted no doubt by the luminosity of Moreau's figures.

Provenance: A label pasted on the stretcher states that the work was purchased from the artist at his New York studio in 1906, but no buyer is designated; Mrs. Doppler, the late wife of the present owner, purchased it in the art market sometime before 1935.

42 VIRGIN AND CHILD
oil on canvas, 8 x 6½ (20.3 x 16.5)
Present location unknown

Provenance: Joseph Jefferson, New York (1906); Jefferson sale, American Art Association, New York, April 27, 1906, no. 3, to Macbeth Gallery, New York; possibly the same work included in the Henry Ward Ranger sale, American Art Association, New York, 1st evening sale, March 29, 1917, no. 1, under title *Madonna and Child,* 8 x 6 inches, signed at lower left, to Le Roy Ireland, New York, to the late William T. Cresmer, Chicago, 1941.

Related Works: Mother and Child, cat. no. 106.

Secular Subjects

43 ARIADNE *figure 62*
oil on canvas, 14 x 24 (35.5 x 61)
Signed: R L Newman, lower right
Present location unknown

Provenance: John Gellatly, New York (1894), probably purchased from the artist; Macbeth Gallery, New York (1919); sale, Lanthier et al, American Art Association, New York, 2d evening sale, April 16, 1919, no. 157, to R. Ederheimer; Michel Michelotti, New York (1953).

References: Knoedler 1894, no. 29; Boston 1894, no. 23.

44 AT THE SPRING *figure 1*
oil on canvas, 20 x 16 (50.8 x 40.7)
Signed: R L Newman 1897, lower left
Museum of Art, Carnegie Institute, Pittsburgh. Anonymous gift, 1971

Provenance: Mrs. Alma Quint, purchased by her father from the artist; Milch Galleries, New York; Babcock Galleries, New York; Joseph Katz, Baltimore; Victor D. Spark, New York.

References: Graham 1961, no. 26, under title *Mother and Nude Child.*

45 THE ATTACK, A STUDY *figure 32*
oil on canvas, 10¼ x 14¼ (26 x 36.2)
Signed: R L Newman, lower right
Mrs. Walter Sharp, Brentwood, Tennessee

Provenance: James S. Inglis, New York, purchased from the artist (1907); Inglis sale, American Art Association, New York, March 9, 1910, no. 71, to William Macbeth, New York; B. B. Jones, Boston, 1910, passed on to Miss Ruth Jones; Ferargil Galleries, New York (1942); Victor D. Spark, New York; Joseph Katz, Baltimore; Sidney A. Levyne, Baltimore; Vose Galleries, Boston; Walter Sharp, Nashville, Tenn., 1954.

References: Virginia 1942, no. 5, under title *St. George and the Dragon;* University of Maryland Art Gallery, College Park, *American Pupils of Thomas Couture,* exhibition, March 19–April 26, 1970, no. 33, illus. p. 56; Albert Boime, "Newman, Ryder, Couture," *American Art Journal* 3 (Fall 1971): fig. 7.

46 THE ATTACK
oil on canvas, 12 x 18 (30.5 x 45.7)
Signed: R L Newman, lower left
Mr. and Mrs. Alfred H. Barr, Jr., New York

Provenance: Cottier & Co., New York (1894); George A. Hearn, New York, 1894; Hearn sale, American Art Association, New York, February 25, 1918, no. 9, illus., to Harold Somers, New York; Somers sale, Parke-Bernet Galleries, New York, May 26, 1943, no. 5, to Frank K. M. Rehn, New York; present owners, 1944.

References: Knoedler 1894, no. 18; Boston 1894, no. 87; New York, Museum of Modern Art, *Romantic Painting in America,* by J. T. Soby and D. C. Miller (New York, 1943), no. 155; *Hundert Jahre amerikanische Malerei 1800–1900,* exhibition, Städelsches Kunstinstitut, Frankfurt, March 14–May 5, 1953, et al (Munich, 1953), no. 70; Tennessee Fine Arts Center, Nashville, *Tennessee Painting: The Past,* exhibition, May 22–July 31, 1960, no. 35; New York, Public Education Association, *The American Vision: Paintings 1825–1875,* exhibition, October 8–November 2, 1968, M. Knoedler & Co., New York, et al, no. 21, illus.

47 BABES IN THE WOODS
oil on canvas, 16 x 20 (40.6 x 50.8)
Signed: R L Newman, lower right
Mr. and Mrs. Milton Horn, Chicago

Provenance: Probably the work of this title lent by Miss Walker to the exhibition at the Knoedler Gallery, New York, in 1894, no. 91; New York art market, to the present owners, about 1936.

48 THE BATHER
oil on canvas, 9 x 7 (22.9 x 17.8)
Miss Rosamond Gilder, New York

Provenance: Richard Watson Gilder, New York, gift or purchase from the artist; passed on to his daughter, the present owner.

Related Works: The Bather, cat. no. 166.

49 THE BATHER
oil on canvas, 7¾ x 10 (19.7 x 25.4)
Signed: R L Newman, lower left
Mr. Herman Abromson, Rockville Centre, New York

Provenance: Probably the work of the same title purchased from the artist by Robert Underwood Johnson, New York (1894).

50 THE BATHER
oil on canvas, 9 x 13⅝ (22.9 x 34.6)
Signed: R L Newman, lower left
Present location unknown

Provenance: Sir William C. Van Horne, Montreal (1894), probably purchased from the artist and passed on to his daughter Miss Adaline Van Horne, who bequeathed it to the Montreal Museum of Fine Arts, 1945; New York art market, to Joseph Katz, Baltimore (1954).

References: Knoedler 1894, no. 85; Boston 1894, no. 68; Graham 1961, no. 19; *Arts* 36 (November 1961): illus. p. 46.

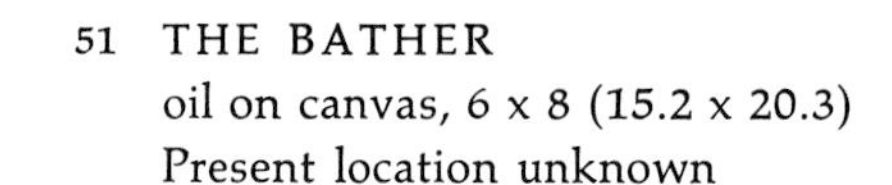

51 THE BATHER
oil on canvas, 6 x 8 (15.2 x 20.3)
Present location unknown

Provenance: John Gellatly, New York (1894), probably purchased from the artist; Frank K. M. Rehn, New York, 1919.

References: Knoedler 1894, no. 34; Boston 1894, no. 28; Rehn 1924, no. 5.

52 THE BIRD
oil on canvas, 18 x 22 (45.7 x 55.9)
Signed: R L Newman 1898, lower left
Present location unknown

Since no photograph of this work exists, a copy of the painting, believed to have been made by Margery Ryerson, is reproduced. The copy, oil on paper, 3 x 4½ inches, was formerly in the possession of Frederic Fairchild Sherman, Westport, Connecticut, and is now owned by Mrs. Sherman's niece, Mrs. Linda Hicks Deftos, Del Mar, California.

Provenance: William T. Evans, New York (1900), probably purchased from the artist; Evans sale, American Art Association, New York, 2d evening sale, February 1, 1900, no. 135, to Frank H. Scott; passed on to his widow who still had it in 1936.

References: Wadsworth Atheneum, Hartford, *Paintings in Hartford Collections,* exhibition, 1936, no. 112, under title *There.*

53 BROTHER AND SISTER *figure 59*
oil on canvas, 9 x 7 (22.9 x 17.8)
Signed: R L Newman, lower left
Mrs. William Penn Cresson, Stockbridge, Massachusetts

Provenance: Daniel Chester French, New York (1898), purchased from the artist and presented to his daughter, the present owner.

References: Whitney 1935, no. 41.

Related Works: Landscape with Figures, fig. 60, cat. no. 93.

54 BROTHER AND SISTER
oil on canvas, 8 x 6 (20.3 x 15.2)
Present location unknown

Provenance: Sir William C. Van Horne, Montreal, purchased from the artist and passed on to his daughter Miss Adaline Van Horne (1934).

Related Works: Landscape with Figures, fig. 60, cat. no. 93.

55 BOY IN THE FIELD
oil on board, 7 x 11 (17.8 x 28)
Signed
Present location unknown

Provenance: Francis Lathrop, New York (1894), purchased from the artist; Lathrop sale, Anderson Art Galleries, New York, 2d evening sale, April 5, 1911, no. 127.

References: Knoedler 1894, no. 68; Boston 1894, no. 53.

56 THE BUTTERFLY
oil on canvas, 6 x 8 (15.2 x 20.3)
Present location unknown

Provenance: William F. Clarke, New York (1894); Nicholas H. Weitzner, Scarsdale, New York; Babcock Galleries, New York; Henry Schulman; Babcock Galleries, New York; Sidney A. Levyne, Baltimore; Babcock Galleries, New York, to the late Roger S. Phillips, Greenwich, Connecticut (1953).

References: Knoedler 1894, no. 17; Boston 1894, no. 13.

57 THE BUTTERFLIES
oil on canvas, 8 x 10 (20.3 x 25.4)
Mr. Sol Wilson, New York

Provenance: Sale, Plaza Art Galleries, New York, 1944, to Babcock Galleries, New York, to the present owner, 1945.

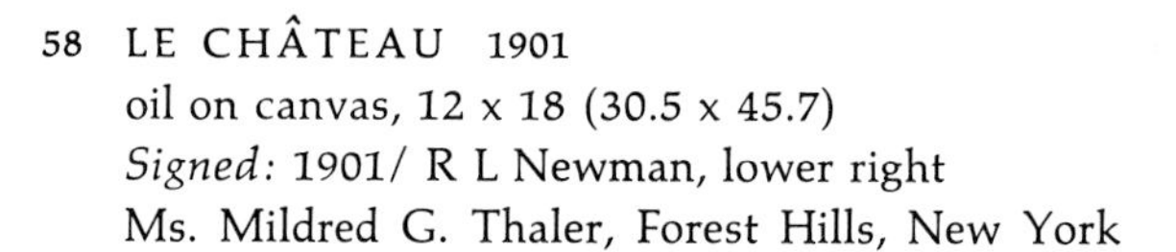

58 LE CHÂTEAU 1901
oil on canvas, 12 x 18 (30.5 x 45.7)
Signed: 1901/ R L Newman, lower right
Ms. Mildred G. Thaler, Forest Hills, New York

This is the only known work by Newman that depicts an actual site; the site, however, has not been identified.

Provenance: John Pierce, Milton, Massachusetts, 1953; sale, Plaza Art Galleries, New York, May 18, 1972, to the present owner.

59 CHILDREN PLAYING *figure 49*
oil on canvas, 10 x $14\frac{1}{2}$ (25.4 x 36.9)
The Brooklyn Museum, Brooklyn, New York (18.28.19)

Provenance: Nestor Sanborn, Brooklyn, New York, probably purchased from the artist, sold to the present owner, 1918.

References: Brooklyn Museum, *Works by American Painters 1860–1885,* exhibition, November 1–29, 1917, no. 60; Whitney 1935, no. 19; Grant Code, "American Painting in the Collection of the Brooklyn Museum," *Brooklyn Museum Quarterly* 24 (April 1937): illus. p. 60; Virginia 1942, no. 19, pl. 7; Albert Boime, "Newman, Ryder, Couture," *American Art Journal* 3 (Fall 1971): fig. 21.

Related Works: The Mystery, fig. 50, cat. no. 118.

60 CHILDREN PLAYING
oil on canvas, 12 x 22 (30.5 x 55.9)
Mrs. William Penn Cresson, Stockbrige, Massachusetts

Provenance: Daniel Chester French, New York, purchased from the artist and passed on to his daughter, the present owner.

Related Works: The Mystery, fig. 50, cat. no. 118.

61 CHILDREN PLAYING
oil on canvas, $7\frac{5}{16}$ x $9\frac{5}{16}$ (18.5 x 23.6)
Signed: R L Newman, lower left
Hopkins Center Art Galleries, Dartmouth College, Hanover, New Hampshire

Provenance: John Gellatly, New York (1894); Miss Elizabeth Scarborough, passed on to Mrs. John Kendrick Bang, New York; Frank K. M. Rehn, New York (1935); Vose Galleries, Boston, 1961; Nicholas H. Weitzner, Scarsdale, New York, 1961; Schweitzer Gallery, New York, to present owner, 1970.

References: Knoedler 1894, no. 25; Boston 1894, no. 19; Whitney 1935, no. 15.

Related Works: The Mystery, fig. 50, cat. no. 118.

62 CHRYSANTHEMUMS
oil on canvas, $29\frac{3}{4}$ x 25 (75.5 x 63.5)
The Virginia Museum of Fine Arts, Richmond. Gift of the Commonwealth of Virginia, 1944 (44.16.2)

Provenance: John Gellatly, New York (1894); Frank K. M. Rehn, New York, 1919; Miss Elizabeth Scarborough (1926), passed on to Mrs. John Kendrick Bang, New York; Frank K. M. Rehn, New York (1935), to present owner, 1944.

References: Knoedler 1894, no. 35; Boston 1894, no. 29; Rehn 1924, no. 1; Whitney 1935, no. 43; M. E. Landgren, "Robert Loftin Newman," *American Magazine of Art* 28 (March 1935): illus. p. 135; Knoedler 1939, no. 28; Virginia 1942, no. 1, pl. 12; *Art News,* February 1–14, 1942, illus. p. 8; New York, Museum of Modern Art, *Romantic Painting in America,* by J. T. Soby and D. C. Miller (New York, 1943), no. 154; W. H. Gerdts and Russell Burke, *American Still-Life Painting* (New York, 1971), p. 193, fig. 13-11.

Related Works: A pastel of the same subject, *Chrysanthemum Studies,* now lost, was lent by Gellatly to the Knoedler exhibition of 1894, no. 37.

63 EVENING
oil on canvas, 14 x 23 (35.5 x 58.5)
Mrs. Walter Sharp, Brentwood, Tennessee

Provenance: C. T. Mott (1894); Charles Erskine Scott Wood, San Francisco (1946); Wood et al sale, Parke-Bernet Galleries, New York, February 2–21, 1946, no. 51, to Babcock Galleries, New York, to present owner, 1954.

References: Knoedler 1894, no. 72; Boston 1894, no. 56; *Art Digest,* April 1, 1947, illus. p. 13, under title *The Witching Hour.*

64 THE FLORAL OFFERING
oil on canvas, 8 x 6 (20.3 x 15.2)
Present location unknown

Provenance: John Gellatly, New York (1894), probably purchased from the artist; Miss Elizabeth Scarborough, passed on to Mrs. John Kendrick Bang, New York; Mrs. George H. Davis, New York (1935).

References: Knoedler 1894, no. 28; Boston 1894, no. 22; Rehn 1924, no. 23; Whitney 1935, no. 7.

65 FIGURE PIECE
oil on canvas, 8¼ x 6¼ (21 x 15.9)
Signed: R L Newman, lower right
Vassar College Art Gallery, Poughkeepsie, New York. Gift of Mrs. Lloyd Williams in memory of her father, Daniel Cottier (40.1.10)

References: Vassar College Art Gallery, *Selections from the Permanent Collection* (Poughkeepsie, New York, 1967), p. 42.

66 THE FORTUNE TELLER *figure 56*
oil on canvas, 18 x 21 (45.7 x 53.3)
Mr. Victor D. Spark, New York

References: Graham 1961, no. 5.

Related Works: The Sibyl, cat. no. 142; *The Fortune Teller,* cat. no. 171.

67 THE FORTUNE TELLER 1887
oil on canvas, 22 x 27 (56 x 68.5)
Signed: R L Newman 1887, lower left
Graham Gallery, New York

Provenance: Thomas McGuinness, Philadelphia (1902); McGuinness sale, J. F. O'Brien, New York, February 5, 1902, no. 31; sale, American paintings, Fifth Avenue Art Galleries, New York, February 19–20, 1903, no. 110, to Louis Katz, New York; C. F. Street; E. C. Babcock, New York (1935); Joseph Katz, Baltimore, 1943, to present owner (1961).

References: London Studio 7 (May 1934): illus. p. 275, under title *The Witch of Endor;* Whitney 1935, no. 8, under title *The Witch of Endor;* Knoedler 1939, no. 29, under title *The Witch of Endor;* Virginia 1942, no. 10, under title *The Witch of Endor;* Graham 1961, no. 23, under title *Three Witches.*

Related Works: The Sibyl, cat. no. 142; *The Fortune Teller,* cat. no. 171.

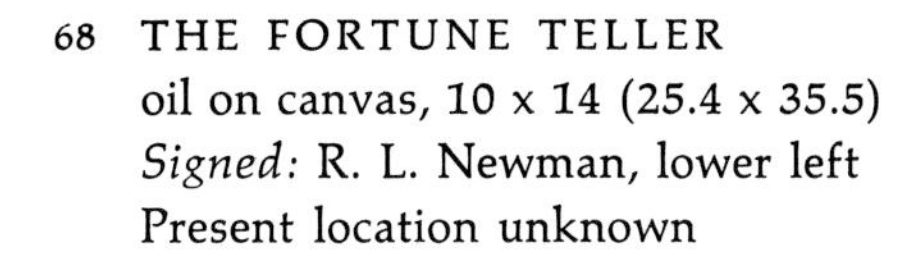

68 THE FORTUNE TELLER
oil on canvas, 10 x 14 (25.4 x 35.5)
Signed: R. L. Newman, lower left
Present location unknown

Provenance: Mrs. Richard K. Maguire, Brooklyn, New York, purchased at Mrs. Nestor Sanborn's studio in 1908 or 1909 and passed on to her son, Richard K. Maguire.

References: Whitney 1935, no. 31; Knoedler 1939, no. 40; Virginia 1942, no. 24.

Related Works: The Sibyl, cat. no. 142; *The Fortune Teller,* cat. no. 171.

69 THE FORTUNE TELLER *figure 74*
oil on canvas, 10 x 14 (25.4 x 35.5)
Signed: R L Newman, lower right
The Metropolitan Museum of Art, New York. Gift of Mrs. Wallace Sawyer, 1921

Provenance: Wallace Sawyer, New York, probably purchased from the artist.

References: New York, Metropolitan Museum of Art, *Catalogue of Paintings,* by Bryson Burroughs, 9th ed. (New York, 1931), p. 263; Whitney 1935, no. 50; M. E. Landgren, "Robert Loftin Newman," *American*

Magazine of Art 28 (March 1935): illus. p. 137; Virginia 1942, no. 15, pl. 5; New York, Museum of Modern Art, *Romantic Painting in America,* by J. T. Soby and D. C. Miller (New York, 1943), no. 156, illus. p. 80.

Related Works: The Prophecy, cat. no. 128; fig. 61, cat. no. 129.

70 THE FORTUNE TELLER *figure 46*
oil on canvas, 10 x 12 (25.4 x 30.5)
Signed: R L Newman, lower left
The Brooklyn Museum, Brooklyn, New York (18.30)

Provenance: Nestor Sanborn, Brooklyn, New York, probably purchased from the artist, to present owner, 1918.

References: Brooklyn Museum, *Works of American Painters 1860–1885,* exhibition, November 1–29, 1917, no. 61; Whitney 1935, no. 53.

Related Works: The Prophecy, cat. no. 128; fig. 61, cat. no. 129.

71 THE FORTUNE TELLER
oil on canvas, 12¼ x 18¼ (31.1 x 46.3)
Present location unknown

Provenance: Lee Woodward Zeigler, purchased from the artist; Frank K. M. Rehn, New York, 1934, later returned to original owner.

References: Whitney 1935, no. 26.

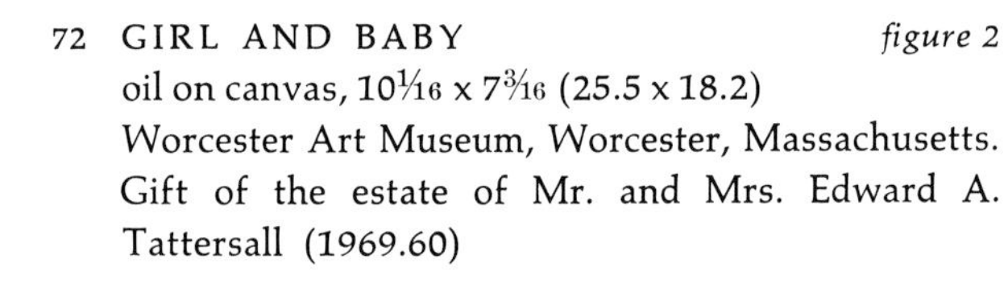

72 GIRL AND BABY *figure 2*
oil on canvas, 10 1/16 x 7 3/16 (25.5 x 18.2)
Worcester Art Museum, Worcester, Massachusetts. Gift of the estate of Mr. and Mrs. Edward A. Tattersall (1969.60)

Provenance: Mrs. Roswell Smith, New York (1894), to Charles T. Yerkes, Chicago, 1894, passed on to his adopted daughter Miss Emilie Grigsby; Grigsby sale, Anderson Galleries, New York, 8th session, January 25, 1912, no. 1128, under title *Woman and a Baby,* to Vose Galleries, Boston; D. B. Logan, 1917; Mr. and Mrs. Edward A. Tattersall, Worcester, Massachusetts.

References: Knoedler 1894, no. 82; Boston 1894, no. 80; *Gazette des beaux-arts,* 6th ser. 75 (February 1970): illus. supp. p. 83.

73 GIRL AND TWO CHILDREN *figure 58*
oil on canvas, 12 x 6 (30.5 x 15.3)
Mrs. Walter Sharp, Brentwood, Tennessee

Provenance: Rufus W. Weeks, New York (1894), purchased from the artist and passed on to his daughter Mrs. Alfred S. Taylor, New York (1935); Babcock Galleries, New York, 1954, to Walter Sharp, Nashville, Tennessee.

References: Knoedler 1894, no. 87; Boston 1894, no. 70; Whitney 1935, no. 3, illus. p. 21.

Related Works: The Holy Family, fig. 18, cat. no. 25; *Madonna and Child,* cat. no. 180.

74 GIRL AT SPRING 1902?
oil on canvas, 12¼ x 10⅛ (31 x 25.5)
Signed: R L Newman 1902?, lower right
Mr. Lee B. Anderson, New York

Provenance: Macbeth Gallery, New York, to Louis Katz, New York, 1916.

Related Works: Woman at the Spring, cat. no. 153.

75 GIRL AT THE WELL
oil on canvas, 10¼ x 6 (26 x 15.2)
Present location unknown

Provenance: Probably the work of the same title owned by Mrs. George Buckham (1894); Albert Milch, New York, to Le Roy Ireland, New York, about 1930.

References: Knoedler 1894, no. 73?; Boston 1894, no. 57?

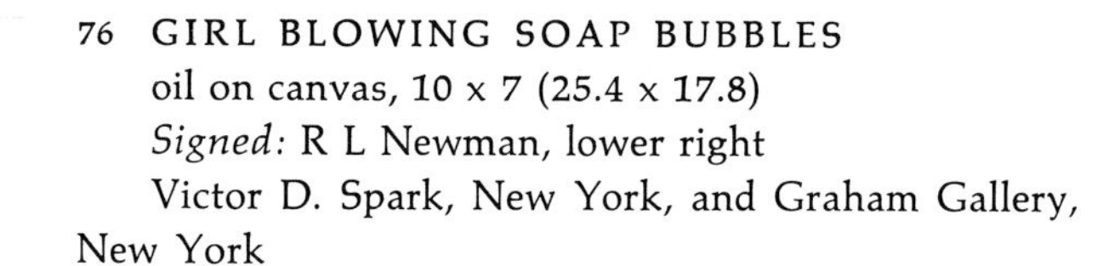

76 GIRL BLOWING SOAP BUBBLES
oil on canvas, 10 x 7 (25.4 x 17.8)
Signed: R L Newman, lower right
Victor D. Spark, New York, and Graham Gallery, New York

Provenance: H. Augustus Lukeman, Stockbridge, Massachusettes, purchased from the artist and passed on to his widow (1935); Victor D. Spark, New York, to Joseph Katz, Baltimore (1954).

References: Graham 1961, no. 4.

77 GIRL BLOWING SOAP BUBBLES *figure 66*
oil on canvas, 20 x 16 (50.8 x 40.6)
Signed: R L Newman, lower left
The Corcoran Gallery of Art, Washington, D.C. (48.55)

Provenance: Frederic Fairchild Sherman, Westport, Connecticut (1916); Sherman sale, Parke-Bernet Galleries, New York, June 4, 1942, no. 20; Babcock Galleries, New York (1945); Vose Galleries, Boston, 1948, sold to present owner, 1948.

References: F. F. Sherman, "Robert Loftin Newman," in his *Landscape and Figure Painters of America* (New York, 1917), illus. facing p. 20, reprinted from *Art in America* 4 (April 1916): 177–84; Whitney 1935, no. 18; George Walter Vincent Smith Art Gallery, Springfield, Massachusetts, *A Showing of the Private Collection of Mr. and Mrs. Frederic Fairchild Sherman,* March 31–May 4, 1941, no. 51, illus.; Virginia 1942, no. 29, pl. 17; American-British Art Center, New York, *Other Worlds,* exhibition, October 8–27, 1945, no. 20; H. B. Caldwell, "A Romantic Painting by Newman," *Corcoran Gallery of Art Bulletin* 3 (January 1951): 13–16, illus. p. 14; Corcoran Gallery of Art, *Catalogue of the Collection of American Paintings,* vol. 1, *Painters Born Before 1850* (Washington, 1966), p. 123, illus.; Albert Boime, "Newman, Ryder, Couture," *American Art Journal* 3 (Fall 1971): fig. 1.

78 GIRL BRINGING HOME A NEW BORN LAMB
oil on canvas, 14 x 8 (35.5 x 20.3)
Signed: R L Newman 1886, lower right
Present location unknown

A solitary figure of a stocky peasant girl, wrapped in a hooded blue cloak, carries in her arms a newborn lamb. She comes toward the spectator, walking toward the right, and is seen vaguely, as in a mist.

Provenance: John Gellatly, New York (1894), probably purchased from the artist; Lanthier et al sale, American Art Association, New York, 2d evening sale, April 16, 1919, no. 125, to M. Knoedler & Co., New York.

References: Knoedler 1894, no. 33; Boston 1894, no. 27.

79 GIRL IN RED
oil on canvas, 13 x 9 (33 x 22.8)
Signed: R L Newman, left
Present location unknown

Provenance: Benjamin Altman, New York, 1902; Macbeth Gallery, New York; Charles B. Lawson, 1906; Lawson sale, American Art Association, New York, 1st evening sale, February 19, 1912, no. 11, to David Belasco, New York; Babcock Galleries, New York, purchased at Leigh's Art Shop, New York, 1944, to the late Roger S. Phillips, Greenwich, Connecticut (1953).

80 GIRLS PLAYING WITH A DOLL
oil on canvas, 7 x 10 (17.8 x 25.4)
Signed: R L Newman, lower left
Mrs. Stedman Buttrick, Concord, Massachusetts

Provenance: Daniel Chester French, New York, purchased from the artist and presented to his cousin George S. Keyes; passed on to the latter's daughter, the present owner.

81 GIRLS READING
oil on canvas, 7 x 10 (17.8 x 25.4)
Signed: R L Newman, lower left
The Brooklyn Museum, Brooklyn, New York (18.31)

Provenance: Nestor Sanborn, Brooklyn, New York, probably purchased from the artist (1917), sold to present owner, 1918.

References: Brooklyn Museum, *Works of American Painters 1860–1885*, exhibition, November 1–29, 1917, no. 59; Whitney 1935, no. 21; Knoedler 1939, no. 22.

82 GIRLS READING
oil on canvas, 6 x 8 (15.3 x 20.3)
Mrs. George W. Remaily, Hammondsport, New York

Provenance: Alexander W. Drake, New York, purchased from the artist and presented to his son-in-law Clifton Wheeler; passed on to the latter's daughter, the present owner.

83 THE GREEK SHEPHERD *figure 54*
oil on canvas, 10 x 12¼ (25.4 x 31)
Montgomery Museum of Fine Arts, Montgomery, Alabama

Provenance: Francis Lathrop, New York (1894), purchased from the artist; Lathrop sale, Anderson Art Galleries, New York, April 4, 1911, no. 35; Macbeth Gallery, New York (1918); Lanthier et al sale, American Art Association, New York, April 16, 1919, no. 42, to Salvatore A. Guarino; Arthur F. Egner, South Orange, New Jersey (1924); Egner sale, Parke-Bernet Galleries, New York, May 4, 1945, no. 40, under title *The Shepherd Boy,* to Babcock Galleries, New York; Joseph Katz, Baltimore; Victor D. Spark and Graham Gallery, New York (1961).

References: Knoedler 1894, no. 69; Boston 1894, no. 54; Rehn 1924, no. 30; Virginia 1942, no. 33; Graham 1961, no. 10, under title *Greek Shepherd Boy.*

84 GROUP OF CHILDREN
oil on canvas, 10 x 14 (25.4 x 35.5)
Present location unknown

Two young girls in yellow, red, and blue costumes are seated on an embankment with a small flaxen-haired child in yellow frock standing before them.

Provenance: John Gellatly, New York (1894), probably purchased from the artist; Ball et al sale, American Art Association, New York, 1st evening sale, March 13, 1919, no. 17, to Arthur F. Egner, South Orange, New Jersey; Egner sale, Parke-Bernet Galleries, New York, May 4, 1945, no. 78.

References: Knoedler 1894, no. 31; Boston 1894, no. 25; Rehn 1924, no. 9; Virginia 1942, no. 34.

85 GROUP OF THREE CHILDREN
oil on canvas, 8 x 10 (20.4 x 25.4)
Signed
Present location unknown

Provenance: Francis Lathrop, New York (1894), purchased from the artist; Lathrop sale, Anderson Art Galleries, New York, 2d evening sale, April 5, 1911, no. 129, under title *A Group of Children Playing.*

References: Knoedler 1894, no. 67.

86 HARVEST TIME
oil on canvas, 7 x 10 (17.8 x 25.4)
Signed
Mr. Herman Abromson, Rockville Centre, New York

Provenance: Francis Lathrop, New York (1894), purchased from the artist; Lathrop sale, Anderson Art Galleries, New York, 1st evening sale, April 4, 1911, no. 60.

References: Knoedler 1894, no. 64.

87 HEAD OF A GIRL *figure 67*
oil on canvas, 10 x 8 (25.4 x 20.3)
The Brooklyn Museum, Brooklyn, New York (18.32)

Provenance: William Merritt Chase, New York (1894), purchased from the artist; Stanford White, New York (1906); White sale, American Art Association, New York, 1st evening sale, April 11, 1907, no. 9, to Nestor Sanborn, Brooklyn, New York, to the present owner, 1918.

References: Knoedler 1894, no. 13; Boston 1894, no. 10; Brooklyn Museum, *Works of American Painters 1860–1885,* exhibition, November 1–29, 1917, no. 58; Whitney 1935, no. 1; Knoedler 1939, no. 23; Albert Boime, "Newman, Ryder, Couture," *American Art Journal,* 3 (Fall 1971): fig. 16; T. B. Brumbaugh, "Letters of Robert Loftin Newman," *Tennessee Historical Quarterly* 32 (Summer 1973): illus. p. 115.

88 IN CONFIDENCE[?]
oil on canvas, 6 x 9 (15.2 x 22.9)
Signed: R L Newman, lower left
Present location unknown

Provenance: Fragments of a review of the Knoedler exhibition of 1894 remain on the back of the original frame, suggesting that the work was included in that exhibition. The subject suggests that it may be the work entitled *In Confidence* lent by Cyrus O. Baker, New York, no. 4. The work reappeared in the possession of Joseph Katz, Baltimore, 1951, and was in the possession of the Graham Gallery, New York, by 1961.

References: Knoedler 1894, no. 4?; Boston 1894, no. 3?; Graham 1961, no. 15, under title *Two Boys in a Landscape.*

Related Works: Red Ridinghood, cat. no. 133, in which the same two figures appear; there is, however, no red cloak in the present work—the cloak draping the figure to the left is yellow-brown and that draping the figure to the right is turquoise-blue.

89 IN THE WOODS
oil on canvas, 7½ x 5½ (19 x 14)
Present location unknown

Provenance: Samuel A. Chapin, New York (1894), purchased from the artist.

References: Knoedler 1894, no. 14; Boston 1894, no. 11.

90 THE JEWEL
oil on canvas, 9 x 7 (22.9 x 17.8)
Present location unknown

Provenance: Mrs. Frank H. Holden, New York (1935), probably purchased from the artist by her father, Robert Underwood Johnson; New York art market, to Joseph Katz, Baltimore (1953); Graham Gallery, New York (1961).

References: Whitney 1935, no. 57; Graham 1961, no. 14, under title *Nude by a Stream.*

91 KNEELING WOMAN
oil on canvas, 10 x 14 (25.4 x 35.5)
Signed: R L Newman, lower right
Present location unknown

A woman wearing a green skirt disclosing bare feet is kneeling in the foreground, her hands working in the soil; landscape at twilight, a tree in the left background, and a setting sun on the horizon at the right.

Provenance: Francis Lathrop, New York (1894), purchased from the artist; Lathrop sale, Anderson Art Galleries, New York, 2d evening sale, April 5, 1911, no. 125, under title *Woman Kneeling;* Major Edward J. Bowes, New York (1946); Bowes sale, Kende Galleries, New York, November 2, 1946, no. 79.

References: Knoedler 1894, no. 65; Boston 1894, no. 52.

92 LANDSCAPE: THE SLEEPER 1901
oil on canvas, 9 1/16 x 12 1/8 (23 x 31)
Signed: R L Newman 1901, lower left
The Brooklyn Museum, Brooklyn, New York. Gift of Nestor Sanborn, 1918 (18.33)

Provenance: Nestor Sanborn, Brooklyn, New York, probably purchased from the artist.

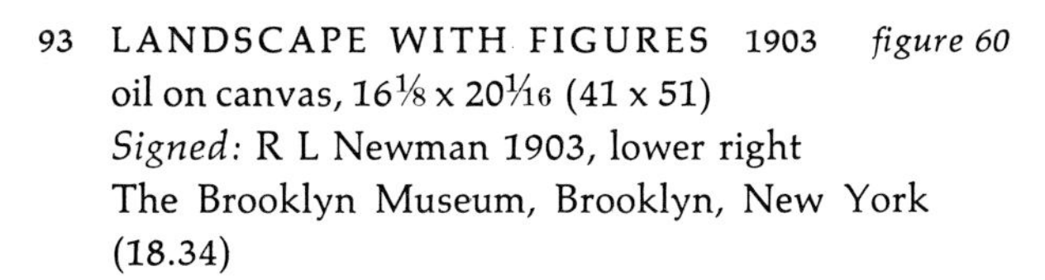

93 LANDSCAPE WITH FIGURES 1903 *figure 60*
oil on canvas, 16 1/8 x 20 1/16 (41 x 51)
Signed: R L Newman 1903, lower right
The Brooklyn Museum, Brooklyn, New York (18.34)

Provenance: Nestor Sanborn, Brooklyn, New York (1917), probably purchased from the artist, sold to present owner, 1918.

References: Brooklyn Museum, Works of American *Painters 1860–1885,* exhibition, November 1–29, 1917, no. 54, under title *Landscape with Woman and Child;* Whitney 1935, no. 40; Virginia 1942, no. 18; T. B. Brumbaugh, "Letters of Robert Loftin Newman," *Tennessee Historical Quarterly* 32 (Summer 1973): illus. p. 114.

Related Works: Brother and Sister, fig. 59, cat. no. 53; cat. no. 54.

94 THE LETTER *figure 76*

oil on canvas, 17¼ x 13¼ (43.8 x 33.7)
Signed: R L Newman, lower left
The Phillips Collection, Washington, D.C.

Provenance: John Gellatly, New York (1894), probably purchased from the artist; Frank K. M. Rehn, New York, 1919, to present owner, 1924.

References: Knoedler 1894, no. 26; Boston 1894, no. 20; Rehn 1924, no. 2; Duncan Phillips, *A Collection in the Making* (New York and Washington, 1926), p. 38, pl. 32; Whitney 1935, no. 6; M. E. Landgren, "Robert Loftin Newman," *American Magazine of Art* 28 (March 1935): illus. p. 138; Knoedler 1939, no. 25; Virginia 1942, no. 16, pl. 3; Phillips Collection, Washington, D.C., *The American Paintings of the Phillips Collection,* exhibition, April 9–May 30, 1944, no. 43; O. W. Larkin, *Art and Life in America* (New York, 1949, rev. & enl. ed., New York, 1960), p. 268, illus. p. 267; David Loeffler Smith, "Romanticism and the American Tradition," *American Artist* 26 (March 1962): illus. p. 33.

95 THE LETTER *figure 14*

oil on canvas, 14 x 12 (35.5 x 30.5)
Victor D. Spark, New York, and Graham Gallery, New York

Provenance: William T. Evans, New York (1898), purchased from the artist; Evans sale, American Art Association, New York, 2d evening sale, February 1, 1900, no. 142, to R. H. Austin; William T. Evans, Montclair, New Jersey (1902); Evans sale, American Art Association, New York, 2d evening sale, April 1, 1913, no. 89, to J. R. Andrews; Andrews sale, American Art Association, New York, 1st evening sale, January 27, 1916, no. 24, illus., to S. G. Rosenbaum; Albert Schwartz; Babcock Galleries, New York; Old Print Shop, New York (1950); Joseph Katz, Baltimore, 1954.

References: Graham 1961, no. 20; W. H. Truettner, "William T. Evans," *American Art Journal* 3 (Fall 1971): 77.

96 THE LETTER *figure 68*
oil on canvas, 8 x 6 (20.3 x 15.2)
Signed: R L Newman, lower left
Dr. and Mrs. Jules Greenwald, Clifton, New Jersey

Provenance: John Gellatly, New York, probably purchased from the artist; Miss Elizabeth Scarborough, passed on to Mrs. John Kendrick Bang, New York; Mrs. George H. Davis, New York (1935); Victor D. Spark, New York, to present owner.

References: Whitney 1935, no. 9.

97 THE LETTER

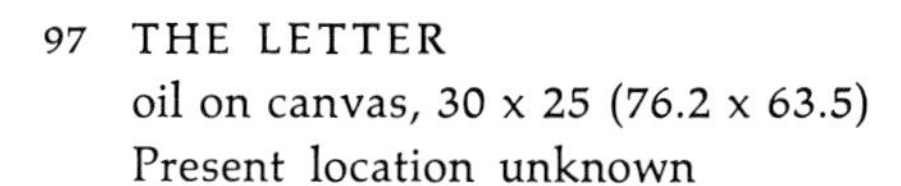

oil on canvas, 30 x 25 (76.2 x 63.5)
Present location unknown

Provenance: Albert Groll, New York, probably purchased at administrator's sale, estate of R. L. Newman, Fifth Avenue Art Galleries, June 6, 1912, no. 10, under title *Woman Reading;* Frank K. M. Rehn, New York, to Arthur F. Egner, South Orange, New Jersey, 1924.

References: Rehn 1924, no. 28; Virginia 1942, no. 36.

98 LITTLE RED RIDINGHOOD

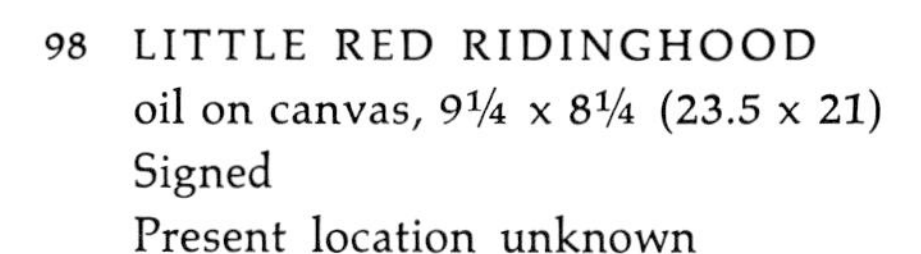

oil on canvas, 9¼ x 8¼ (23.5 x 21)
Signed
Present location unknown

Provenance: Sir William C. Van Horne, Montreal, purchased from the artist and passed on to his daughter Miss Adaline Van Horne (1934).

99 LITTLE RED RIDINGHOOD *figure 29*
oil on canvas, 14¼ x 10¼ (36.2 x 26)
Signed: R L Newman, lower right
Mrs. Nellie C. Bender, Bronxville, New York

Provenance: Rufus W. Weeks, New York, probably purchased from the artist (1894) and passed on to his daughter Mrs. Alfred S. Taylor, New York (1935); Babcock Galleries, New York, to William H. Bender, Jr., 1963.

References: Boston 1894, no. 71; Whitney 1935, no. 10, under title *Red Ridinghood.*

100 LITTLE RED RIDINGHOOD
oil on canvas, 8 x 6 (20.3 x 15.2)
Signed: R L Newman, lower left
Mr. and Mrs. Walter Fillin, Rockville Centre, New York

Provenance: Mrs. Wallace Sawyer, Asbury Park, New Jersey (1924), probably purchased from the artist; Mrs. Frank K. M. Rehn, New York (1935), to present owner.

References: Rehn 1924, no. 25; Whitney 1935, no. 25.

101 LITTLE RED RIDINGHOOD AND THE WOLF *figure 57*
oil on panel, 7⅝ x 11¾ (19.5 x 30)
Museum of Fine Arts, Boston, Massachusetts. Gift, 1917

See also *Red Ridinghood.*

102 THE LOVERS 1889
oil on canvas, 6⅛ x 8½ (15.5 x 21.5)
Signed: R L Newman 1889, lower left
Mrs. George W. Remaily, Hammondsport, New York

Provenance: Alexander W. Drake, New York, 1889, purchased from the artist and passed on, after the death of his widow, to his granddaughter, the present owner.

References: Knoedler 1894, no. 20; Boston 1894, no. 15, Whitney 1935, no. 46.

103 THE LOVERS *figure 41*
oil on canvas, 6 x 8 (15.3 x 20.3)
Signed: R L Newman, lower right
Mr. and Mrs. Marc Nisbet, Woodside, New York

Provenance: Hamilton Galleries, New York, to present owners, 1972.

References: Knoedler 1894, included two unidentified paintings of this title, no. 41 (Boston 1894, no. 31), lent by Helena de Kay Gilder, New York, and no. 93, lent by Miss Mary N. Shepard; Wyatt Eaton also lent a *Young Lovers*, no. 96 (Boston 1894, no. 75).

104 THE LOVERS 1897
oil on canvas, 11 x 16½ (28 x 42)
Signed: R L Newman 1897, lower right
Wadsworth Atheneum, Hartford. The Ella Gallup Sumner and Mary Catlin Sumner Collection (36.48)

Provenance: James Edwin Nichols sale, Clarke's Art Rooms, New York, June 1, 1916, no. 15, to Snedecor and Co., New York; Burton Mansfield (1924); Frank K. M. Rehn, New York, 1924; Macbeth Gallery, New York, 1924; W. W. Drew, 1928; Macbeth Gallery, New York (1935), to present owner, 1936.

References: Rehn 1924, not in catalog; Whitney 1935, no. 44, under title *Romance—The Way to the Enchanted Castle.*

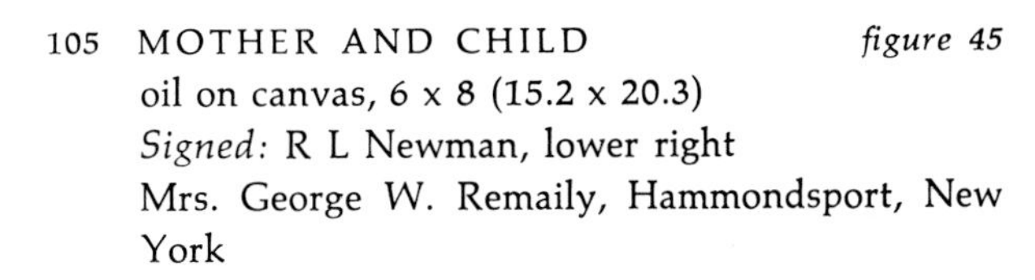

105 MOTHER AND CHILD *figure 45*
oil on canvas, 6 x 8 (15.2 x 20.3)
Signed: R L Newman, lower right
Mrs. George W. Remaily, Hammondsport, New York

Provenance: Alexander W. Drake, New York (1894), purchased from the artist and passed on, after the death of his widow, to his granddaughter, the present owner.

References: Knoedler 1894, no. 19; Boston 1894, no. 14; Knoedler 1939, no. 36.

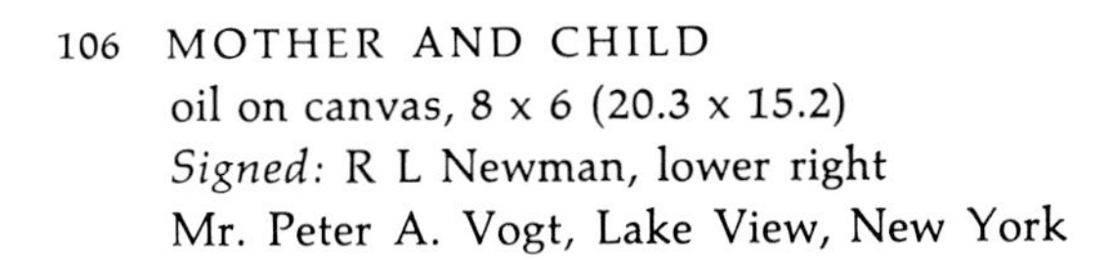

106 MOTHER AND CHILD
oil on canvas, 8 x 6 (20.3 x 15.2)
Signed: R L Newman, lower right
Mr. Peter A. Vogt, Lake View, New York

Provenance: James Welch, Canton, Ohio, to present owner, 1971.

Related Works: Virgin and Child, cat. no. 42.

107 MOTHER AND CHILD 1900
oil on canvas, 17 x 14 (43.2 x 35.5)
Signed: R L Newman 1900, lower left
Art Institute of Chicago. Charles H. and Mary F. S. Worcester Collection

Provenance: Macbeth Gallery, New York (1919); Lanthier et al sale, American Art Association, New York, 2d evening sale, April 16, 1919, no. 139, to Salvatore A. Guarino; J. W. Young, Chicago, to Charles H. Worcester, Chicago, 1921.

References: Virginia 1942, no. 13.

108 MOTHER AND CHILD 1902 *figure 4*
oil on canvas, 18 x 14 (45.7 x 35.5)
Signed: R L Newman 1902, lower right
Private collection, Denver, Colorado

Provenance: Silas Dustin, gift of the artist; Frederic Fairchild Sherman, Westport, Connecticut (1916); Babcock Galleries, New York (1946); Joseph Katz, Baltimore; Graham Gallery, New York (1961), to Mrs. M. J. Hoover, Denver, Colorado, to present owner.

References: F. F. Sherman, "Robert Loftin Newman," in his *Landscape and Figure Painters of America* (New York, 1917), illus. facing p. 16, reprinted from *Art in America* 4 (April 1916): 177–84; Whitney 1935, no. 22; M. E. Landgren, "Robert Loftin Newman," *American Magazine of Art* 28 (March 1935): illus. p. 139; F. F. Sherman, "Robert Loftin Newman," *Art in America* 27 (April 1939): 75; George Walter Vincent Smith Art Gallery, Springfield, Massachusetts, *A Showing of the Private Collection of Mr. and Mrs. Frederic Fairchild Sherman,* March 31–May 4, 1941, no. 52, illus.; Virginia 1942, no. 30, illus. cover; *Art News* 45 (December 1946): illus. p. 47; Graham 1961, no. 12.

109 MOTHER AND CHILD
oil on board, 17 x 13 (43.2 x 33)
Signed: R L Newman, lower right
Victor D. Spark, New York, and Graham Gallery, New York

Provenance: Frank K. M. Rehn, New York (1945); Joseph Katz, Baltimore, 1945.

References: Graham 1961, no. 9, under title *Mother with a Nude Child.*

110 MOTHER AND CHILD *figure 64*
oil on canvas, 10 x 12 (25.4 x 30.5)
Signed: R L Newman, lower right
Mrs. Walter Sharp, Brentwood, Tennessee

Provenance: Rufus W. Weeks, New York, purchased from the artist and passed on to his daughter Mrs. Alfred S. Taylor, New York (1935); Babcock Galleries, New York, 1954, to Walter Sharp, Nashville, Tennessee, 1954.

References: Whitney 1935, no. 17.

Related Works: Mother and Child in Landscape, fig. 65, cat. no. 182.

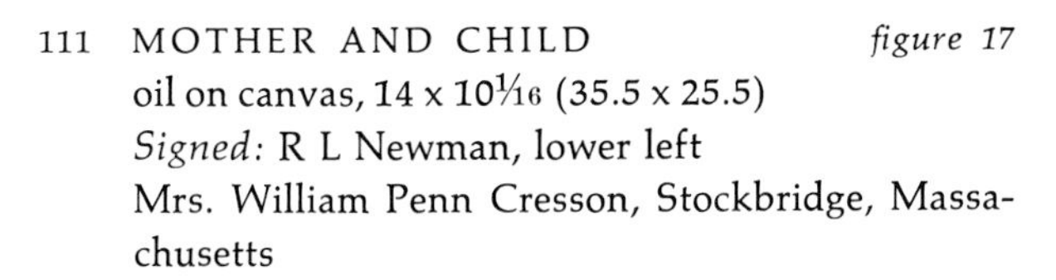

111 MOTHER AND CHILD *figure 17*
oil on canvas, 14 x $10\frac{1}{16}$ (35.5 x 25.5)
Signed: R L Newman, lower left
Mrs. William Penn Cresson, Stockbridge, Massachusetts

Provenance: Daniel Chester French (1898), purchased from the artist and passed on to his daughter, the present owner.

112 MOTHER AND CHILD
oil on canvas, 11¼ x 9¼ (28.6 x 23.5)
Signed: R L Newman, lower right
Mrs. William Penn Cresson, Stockbridge, Massachusetts

Provenance: Daniel Chester French, New York (1898), purchased from the artist and presented to his daughter, the present owner.

References: Society of American Artists, New York, Twenty-first Exhibition, 1899, no. 315; Whitney 1935, no. 55; F. F. Sherman, "Robert Loftin Newman," *Art in America* 27 (April 1939): 75.

113 MOTHER AND CHILD AND GIRL
oil on canvas, 10 x 12 (25.4 x 30.5)
Victor D. Spark, New York, and Graham Gallery, New York

References: Graham 1961, no. 7.

114 MOTHER AND CHILD RESTING ON A BEACH
oil on canvas, 9 x 12⅛ (22.9 x 30.8)
Signed: R L Newman, lower right
Victor D. Spark, New York, and Graham Gallery, New York

Provenance: Newhouse Galleries, New York, to Joseph Katz, Baltimore, 1947.

References: Graham 1961, no. 3, under title *Mother and Child.*

Related Works: A similar work, measuring 9 x 15 inches and unsigned, was once owned by Theron J. Blakeslee, New York, and was offered at the Blakeslee sale, American Art Association, New York, 5th evening sale, March 10, 1916, no. 376, under title *Mother and Child on a Beach,* and was sold to James W. Farnham.

115 MOTHER AND CHILD WITH A BOOK
oil on canvas, 12 x 10 (30.5 x 25.4)
Signed: R L Newman, lower right
Victor D. Spark, New York, and Graham Gallery, New York

Provenance: A. T. Sanden, passed on to his daughter Mrs. E. D. Gurney; Babcock Galleries, New York (1953), to Joseph Katz, Baltimore, 1954.

References: Graham 1961, no. 6.

116 MOTHER AND TWO CHILDREN *figure 12*
oil on canvas, 8¼ x 14¼ (21 x 36.2)
Mrs. Walter Sharp, Brentwood, Tennessee

Provenance: Rufus W. Weeks, New York, purchased from the artist and passed on to his daughter Mrs. Alfred S. Taylor, New York (1935); Babcock Galleries, New York, to Walter Sharp, Nashville, Tennessee, 1954.

References: Whitney 1935, no. 4.

117 MOTHERHOOD
oil on canvas, $5\frac{1}{2}$ x $7\frac{1}{2}$ (14 x 19)
Present location unknown

Provenance: Samuel A. Chapin, New York, purchased from the artist.

118 THE MYSTERY *figure 50*
oil on canvas, 24 x 20 (61 x 50.8)
Signed: R L Newman, lower left
Mr. John Graham II, Mentone, Alabama

Provenance: William T. Evans, New York (1900), probably purchased from the artist; Evans sale, American Art Association, New York, 3d evening sale, February 2, 1900, no. 245, to Harold Godwin, Roslyn, New York; Macbeth Gallery, New York, to Henry Marquand Co., Morgan Hayes & Co., Paris, 1908; sale, Coleman Galleries, New York, September 18, 1941, to present owner.

References: W. H. Truettner, "William T. Evans," *American Art Journal* 3 (Fall 1971): 77.

Related Works: *Children Playing,* fig. 49, cat. nos. 59-61.

119 THE NIGHTINGALE
oil on canvas, $12\frac{1}{8}$ x $9\frac{1}{8}$ (30.8 x 23.2)
Signed: R L Newman, lower left
Graham Gallery, New York

120 THE NIGHTINGALE
oil on canvas, $7\frac{1}{2}$ x $5\frac{1}{2}$ (19 x 14)
Graham Gallery, New York

Provenance: Robert Underwood Johnson, New York (1894), passed on to his daughter Mrs. Frank H. Holden, New York; Joseph Katz, Baltimore.

References: Knoedler 1894, no. 46; Boston 1894, no. 35; Graham 1961, no. 16, under title *Seated Mother and Child.*

121 THE NIGHTINGALE *figure 47*
oil on canvas, 11⅞ x 8⅞ (30.2 x 22.5)
Signed: R L Newman, lower left
Victor D. Spark, New York, and Graham Gallery, New York

Provenance: Theron J. Blakeslee, New York (1916); Blakeslee Galleries sale, American Art Association, New York, March 10, 1916, no. 375, under title *Song of the Birds,* to Holland Art Galleries, New York.

122 NUDE
oil on wood, 2½ x 4⅛ (6.4 x 10.5)
Signed: R L Newman, lower center
Mr. Marchal E. Landgren, Washington, D.C.

Provenance: Painted for and presented to Alexander W. Drake, New York (1894) by the artist in appreciation of Mr. Drake's support of his work. Mrs. Drake presented it to the present owner in the same spirit.

References: Knoedler 1894, no. 22.

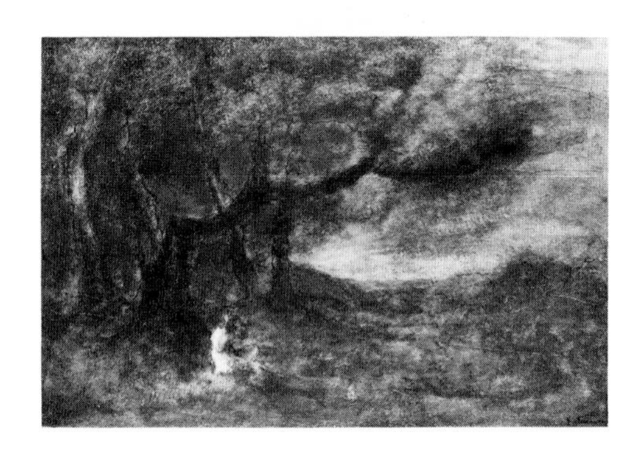

123 PAN IN A FOREST CLEARING
oil on canvas, 12 x 18 (30.5 x 45.7)
Signed: R L Newman, lower right
Victor D. Spark, New York

Provenance: Albert L. Groll, New York, probably purchased from the artist, to George J. Dyer, New York, 1924; Frederic Fairchild Sherman, Westport, Connecticut (1935).

References: Rehn 1924, no. 13, under title *Pan*; Whitney 1935, no. 54, under title *Pan*; George Walter Vincent Smith Art Gallery, Springfield, Massachusetts, *A Showing of the Private Collection of Mr. and Mrs. Frederic Fairchild Sherman,* March 31–May 4, 1941, no. 53; Graham 1961, no. 13, under title *Pan in a Landscape.*

124 THE PEACOCK
oil on canvas, 10 x 16 (25.4 x 40.6)
Signed
Mrs. Hugh C. Thompson, Tucson, Arizona

Provenance: Clarence Clough Buel, New York (1894), purchased from the artist and passed on, after the death of his widow, to his daughter, the present owner.

References: Knoedler 1894, no. 10; Boston 1894, no. 8; Whitney 1935, no. 56; Knoedler 1939, no. 34; Virginia 1942, no. 23.

125 PEASANT GIRL
oil on canvas, 8 x 6 (20.3 x 15.3)
Signed: R L Newman, lower left
Mr. Norton Asner, Baltimore, Maryland

Provenance: Robert Underwood Johnson, New York (1894), purchased from the artist and passed on to his daughter, Mrs. Frank H. Holden, 1937.

References: Knoedler 1894, no. 45; Boston 1894, no. 34.

126 PORTRAIT OF ADELIA BOISSEAU WARFIELD AND DAUGHTER HULDAH BELLE ca. 1857 *figure 10*
oil on canvas, $84\frac{1}{2}$ x 55 (214.5 x 142)
Mr. Leslie Cheek, Jr., Richmond, Virginia

Provenance: Commissioned by the sitters at Clarksville, Tennessee, about 1857, and passed on to the present owner, whose maternal grandmother was Huldah Belle Warfield.

127 PORTRAIT OF WILLIAM WALLACE WARFIELD AND SON *figure 11*
oil on canvas, 85 x 55 (216 x 139.5)
Mr. Leslie Cheek, Jr., Richmond, Virginia

Provenance: Commissioned by the sitters at Clarksville, Tennessee, about 1857, and passed on to the present owner.

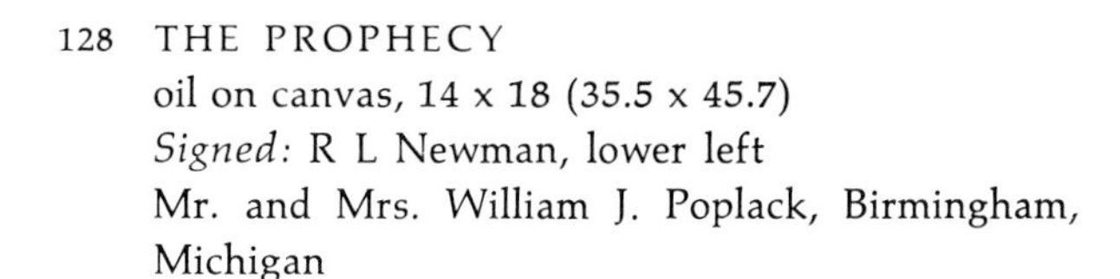

128 THE PROPHECY

oil on canvas, 14 x 18 (35.5 x 45.7)
Signed: R L Newman, lower left
Mr. and Mrs. William J. Poplack, Birmingham, Michigan

Provenance: Nestor Sanborn, Brooklyn, New York, to E. C. Babcock, New York, 1926; Joseph Katz, Baltimore, 1945; Victor D. Spark and Graham Gallery, New York (1961).

References: Whitney 1935, no. 48; Virginia 1942, no. 9, pl. 9; *Art Digest*, May 1, 1945, illus. p. 7; Graham 1961, no. 11.

Related Works: The Fortune Teller, figs. 46, 74, cat. nos. 69, 70.

129 THE PROPHECY *figure 61*

oil on canvas, 25 x 30 (63.5 x 76.2)
Signed: R L Newman, lower left
Addison Gallery of American Art, Phillips Academy, Andover, Massachusetts

Provenance: Mrs. Herschel C. Parker, Brooklyn, New York; Newhouse Galleries, New York; Pell et al sale, Parke-Bernet Galleries, New York, April 18, 1940, no. 31, to Babcock Galleries, New York; present owner, 1943.

References: Lyman Allyn Museum, New London, Connecticut, *American Painting of the Last Fifty Years,* exhibition, 1934, no. 21; Virginia 1942, no. 11, pl. 8; *Addison Gallery of American Art Bulletin,* 1943, pp. 21, 23.

Related Works: The Fortune Teller, figs. 46, 74, cat. nos. 69, 70.

130 PSYCHE *figure 15*

oil on canvas, 9½ x 13½ (24.1 x 34.3)
Signed: R L Newman, lower left
Mr. and Mrs. Walter Fillin, Rockville Centre, New York

Provenance: John Gellatly, New York (1894), purchased from the artist; Miss Elizabeth Scarborough (1924), passed on to Mrs. John Kendrick Bang, New York; Frank K. M. Rehn, New York (1935), to present owners.

References: Knoedler 1894, no. 30; Boston 1894, no. 24; Rehn 1924, no. 29; Whitney 1935, no. 5.

131 PSYCHE
oil on canvas, 8 x 12 (20.3 x 30.5)
Signed
Present location unknown

Provenance: Francis Lathrop, New York (1894), purchased from the artist; Lathrop sale, Anderson Art Galleries, New York, 1st evening sale, April 4, 1911, no. 42.

References: Knoedler 1894, no. 66.

132 RED RIDINGHOOD
oil on canvas, 16 x 13½ (40.6 x 34.3)
Signed: R L Newman, lower right
Victor D. Spark, New York, and Graham Gallery, New York

Provenance: Otto Heinigke, New York, probably purchased from the artist (1894), passed on to his son Otto W. Heinigke, New York; Victor Spark, New York, to Joseph Katz, Baltimore; present owners (1961).

References: Knoedler 1894, no. 43; Boston 1894, no. 33; Graham 1961, no. 18.

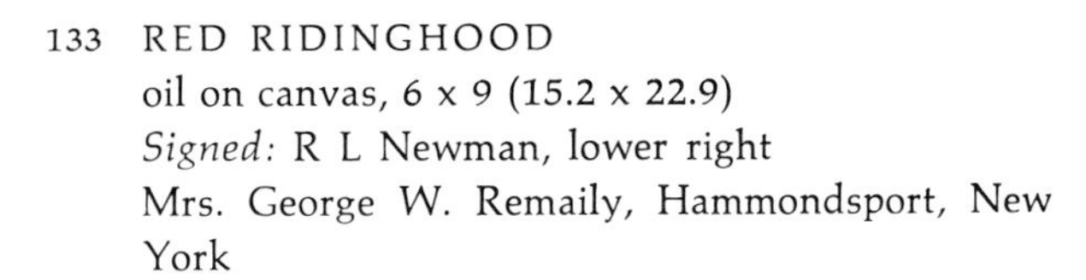

133 RED RIDINGHOOD
oil on canvas, 6 x 9 (15.2 x 22.9)
Signed: R L Newman, lower right
Mrs. George W. Remaily, Hammondsport, New York

Provenance: Alexander W. Drake, New York (1894), purchased from the artist and passed on, after the death of his widow, to his granddaughter, the present owner.

References: Knoedler 1894, no. 21; Boston 1894, no. 16.

Related Works: In Confidence [?], cat. no. 88.

134 RED RIDINGHOOD AND THE WOLF
oil on canvas, 6 x 8 (15.2 x 20.3)
Signed: R L Newman, lower left
Mrs. Walter Sharp, Brentwood, Tennessee

Provenance: Robert Underwood Johnson, New York (1894); William T. Evans, New York, 1894; Robert Underwood Johnson, New York (1935), passed on to his daughter Mrs. Frank H. Holden, New York, 1937; William T. Cresmer, Chicago; Babcock Galleries, New York, to Walter Sharp, Nashville, Tennessee (1953).

References: Knoedler 1894, no. 51; Boston 1894, no. 41; W. H. Truettner, "William T. Evans," *American Art Journal* 3 (Fall 1971): 77.

See also *Little Red Ridinghood.*

135 REST BY THE WAYSIDE
oil on canvas, 6¼ x 10 (15.9 x 25.4)
Mary Washington College, Fredericksburg, Virginia

Provenance: Rufus W. Weeks, New York (1894), purchased from the artist and passed on to his daughter Mrs. Alfred S. Taylor, New York (1935); Milch Galleries, New York (1960), to the present owner, 1960.

References: Boston 1894, no. 72, under title *Wayside Rest;* Whitney 1935, no. 23; Mary Washington College, *Fifth Exhibition of Modern Art,* October 23–November 20, 1960, no. 34, illus.

136 SAPPHO *figure 51*
oil on canvas, 12⅝ x 18⅝ (32 x 47.3)
Victor D. Spark, New York, and Graham Gallery, New York

Provenance: Probably the work of the same title sold by the Macbeth Gallery, New York, to John Gellatly, New York, 1896; Macbeth Gallery, New York (1919); Ball et al sale, American Art Association, New York, 2d evening sale, March 14, 1919, no. 118, to Vose Galleries, Boston; Frank K. M. Rehn, New York, 1927; Joseph Katz, Baltimore, 1944; present owners (1961).

References: Knoedler 1939, no. 26; Graham 1961, no. 1, under title *Seated Woman.*

Related Works: Sappho, cat. no. 186a.

137 SAPPHO 1875 *figure 52*
oil on canvas, 14 x 10 (35.5 x 25.4)
Signed: R L Newman 1875, at left
Mr. and Mrs. I. David Orr, New York

Provenance: Miss A. D. Kittell (1894); E. C. Babcock, New York (1935); Joseph P. Hartert, New York; Louis D'Aras, New York, to presents owners, about 1940.

References: Knoedler 1894, no. 58; Boston 1894, no. 47; Whitney 1935, no. 14.

138 SHEEP *figure 26*

oil on canvas, 14½ x 16 (36.8 x 40.6)
Signed: R L Newman, lower left
The Dayton Art Institute, Dayton, Ohio. Anonymous gift (62.63)

Provenance: George C. Aronstamm, New York, to Frank K. M. Rehn, New York, 1926; Hon. J. William Middendorf II, New York.

References: Whitney 1935, no. 39; Virginia 1942, no. 2.

Related Works: *Sheep,* cat. no. 187.

139 THE SHIPWRECK *figure 34*

oil on canvas, 11 x 23½ (28 x 59.7)
Signed: R L Newman, lower left
The New Britain Museum of American Art, New Britain, Connecticut. Harriet Russell Stanley Fund

Provenance: Michel Michelotti, New York, to Macbeth Gallery, New York, to present owner, 1949.

140 THE SHIPWRECK

oil on canvas, 10 x 14 (25.4 x 35.5)
Present location unknown

Provenance: Administrator's sale, estate of the artist, Fifth Avenue Art Galleries, New York, June 6, 1912, no. 2, to Vose Galleries, Boston.

141 SIBYL

oil on canvas, 11 x 9 (28 x 22.8)
Signed: R L Newman, lower right
Washington County Museum of Fine Arts, Hagerstown, Maryland

Provenance: Probably the work of the same title sold by Theron J. Blakeslee, New York, to R. B. Angus, Montreal, 1894; Thomas R. Ball, New York (1919); Ball sale, American Art Association, New York, March 13–14, 1919, no. 85, to Vose Galleries, Boston; Frank K. M. Rehn, New York, 1924; William F. Laporte, Passaic, New York, 1924; Laporte sale, Parke-Bernet Galleries, New York, March 30, 1944, no. 38, to Joseph Katz, Baltimore; Sidney Levyne, Baltimore (1954).

References: Knoedler 1894, no. 6?; Boston 1894, no. 5?

142 THE SIBYL
oil on canvas, 9¼ x 12¼ (23.5 x 31)
Present location unknown

Provenance: Sir William C. Van Horne, Montreal, purchased from the artist and passed on to his daughter Miss Adaline Van Horne (1934).

Related Works: The subject of the painting is the same as *The Fortune Teller,* figs. 56, 108, 109, cat. nos. 66–68.

143 THE SKYLARK *figure 48*
oil on canvas, 12 x 16 (30.5 x 40.6)
Signed: R L Newman, lower right
Mr. Richard Howes, Knoxville, Tennessee

Provenance: Leon Deutsch, to E. C. Babcock, New York (1939); Gifford Cochran, Palm Beach, Florida, 1939; Vose Galleries, Boston, to present owner, 1972.

References: Knoedler 1939, no. 31, under title *The Gypsies;* Virginia 1942, no. 28, under title *The Gypsies.*

144 THE SKYLARK *figure 77*
oil on canvas, 14 x 18 (35.5 x 45.7)
Signed: R L Newman, lower right
The Phillips Collection, Washington, D.C.

Provenance: Frederic Fairchild Sherman, New York (1924): to present owner, 1924.

References: Rehn 1924, no. 6; Whitney 1935, no. 12; Virginia 1942, no. 17.

145 SYMBOLIC FIGURE
oil on canvas, 14 x 6¼ (35.5 x 16)
Mrs. Linda Hicks Deftos, Del Mar, California

Provenance: Frederic Fairchild Sherman, Westport, Connecticut, passed on to his widow's niece, the present owner.

146 THREE NYMPHS AND A SATYR ca. 1908
oil on canvas, 13 x 16¼ (33 x 41)
Signed: R L Newman, lower right
Norman Lenson, M.D., Brookline, Massachusetts

Provenance: Painted and given to Andrew O'Connor, Jr., at the time Newman was staying at O'Connor's place at Clamart, near Paris, 1908; auction sale, Paxton, Massachusetts, 1921 or 1922, to a private collector, who sold it to the present owner.

147 TIGER AND PREY
oil on canvas, 10 x 14 (25.4 x 35.5)
Signed: R L Newman, lower right
Present location unknown

In a bleak and treeless country with blue mountains in the distance, at nightfall, a tiger on a bank in the foreground is feeding upon a small animal it has struck down; another tiger appears in the distance.

Provenance: John Gellatly, New York (1894), probably purchased from the artist; Lanthier et al sale, American Art Association, New York, 1st evening sale, April 15, 1919, no. 46, to A. Schilling.

References: Knoedler 1894, no. 32; Boston 1894, no. 26.

148 TIGER AT REST *figure 71*
oil on canvas, 8⅛ x 10⅛ (20.6 x 25.9)
Signed: R L Newman, lower right
Present location unknown

Provenance: Robert Underwood Johnson, New York (1894), probably purchased from the artist and passed on to his daughter Mrs. Frank H. Holden, 1937; Joseph Katz, Baltimore, 1953; Graham Gallery, New York, and Victor D. Spark, New York (1961).

References: Knoedler 1894, no. 47; Boston 1894, no. 36; Whitney 1935, no. 11; Graham 1961, no. 22.

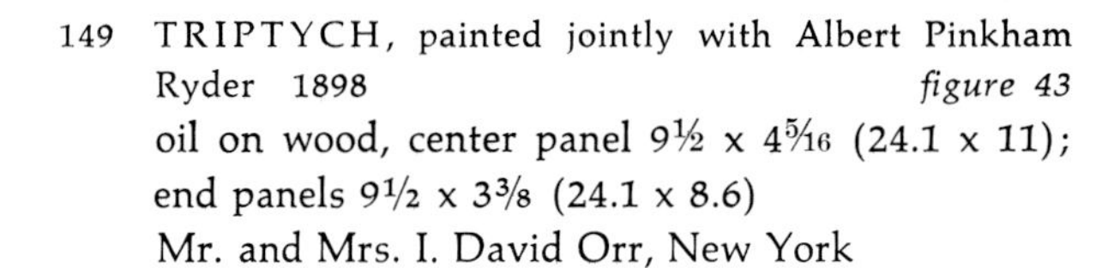

149 TRIPTYCH, painted jointly with Albert Pinkham Ryder 1898 *figure 43*
oil on wood, center panel $9\frac{1}{2} \times 4\frac{5}{16}$ (24.1 x 11); end panels $9\frac{1}{2} \times 3\frac{3}{8}$ (24.1 x 8.6)
Mr. and Mrs. I. David Orr, New York

Inscription: The following inscription is pasted on the back of the center panel: Thumbnail sketches by/ Albert Ryder & R L Newman/done by special request for R. L. Newman/1898/Property Mrs. R. L. Newman/ Murfreesboro, Tenn.

Provenance: Mrs. Robert L. (Mattie Todd) Newman, Murfreesboro, Tennessee, 1898; M. Collins, New York, to the present owners.

150 A TROUBADOR PLAYING A LUTE 1897 *figure 55*
oil on canvas, $11\frac{5}{8} \times 10\frac{1}{4}$ (29.5 x 26)
Signed: R L Newman 1897, lower left
Victor D. Spark, New York, and Graham Gallery, New York

Provenance: Mrs. Alma Quint, purchased from the artist by her father; Milch Galleries, New York; Babcock Galleries, New York (1953), to Joseph Katz, Baltimore.

References: Graham 1961, no. 21, under title *Moonlight Sonata.*

151 WALKING TIGER
oil on canvas, 14 x 24 (35.5 x 61)
Mrs. George W. Remaily, Hammondsport, New York

A tiger, seen in profile, walking toward the left, fills the entire foreground of the painting.

Provenance: Painted for and presented by the artist to Mrs. Henry Fairchild James, sister-in-law of Alexander W. Drake; passed on to Mr. Drake's granddaughter, the present owner.

References: Whitney 1935, no. 30; Knoedler 1939, no. 37.

152 THE WANDERING MIND *figure 16*

oil on canvas, $9\frac{1}{2} \times 12\frac{1}{2}$ (24.1 x 31.8)
Signed: R L Newman, lower right
Present location unknown

Provenance: Sir William C. Van Horne, Montreal, purchased from the artist and passed on to his daughter Miss Adaline Van Horne (1934).

References: F. F. Sherman, "Robert Loftin Newman," in his *Landscape and Figure Painters of America* (New York, 1917), illus. facing p. 14, reprinted from *Art in America* 4 (April 1916): 177–84.

153 WOMAN AT THE SPRING

oil on canvas, $20\frac{1}{4} \times 24\frac{1}{4}$ (51.5 x 61.5)
Signed: R L Newman, lower right
The Newark Museum, Newark, New Jersey. Gift of Mrs. William B. Connett

Provenance: Frederick T. Van Beuren, Morristown, New Jersey, purchased from the artist and presented to Mrs. Connett.

Related Works: *Girl at Spring,* cat. no. 74.

154 WOMAN BATHING BY A WATERFALL

oil on canvas, 16 x 12 (40.6 x 35.5)
Victor D. Spark, New York, and Graham Gallery, New York

Provenance: Huber Clark et al sale, S. T. Freeman & Co., Philadelphia, December 14–15, 1925, no. 73, under title *The Bather.*

References: Graham 1961, no. 28, illus.

155 WOOD AND FIGURES *figure 44*

oil on canvas, $13\frac{3}{4} \times 16\frac{1}{8}$ (35 x 41)
Nebraska Art Association, Lincoln. Nelle Cochrane Woods Collection

Provenance: Robert Underwood Johnson, New York (1894), purchased from the artist and passed on to his daughter Mrs. Frank H. Holden, New York; Macbeth Gallery, New York, to Sidney A. Levyne, Baltimore, 1947; Vose Galleries, Boston, to the present owner, 1959.

References: Knoedler 1894, no. 48; Boston 1894, no. 38; Rehn 1924, no. 22; Knoedler 1939, no. 39; Virginia 1942, no. 3, pl. 11; *Pictures on Exhibit* 5 (February 1942): illus. p. 15.

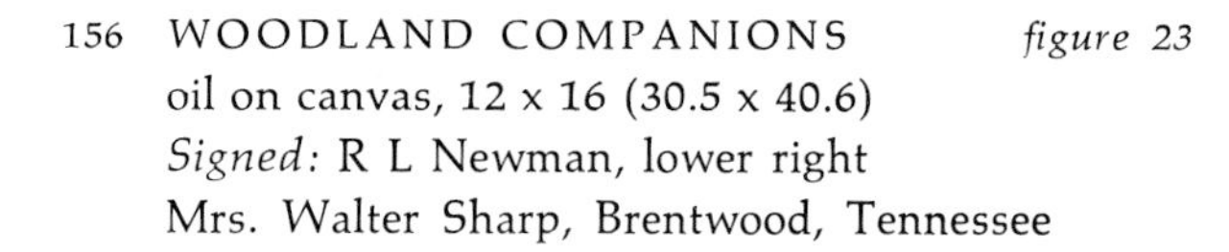

156 WOODLAND COMPANIONS *figure 23*
oil on canvas, 12 x 16 (30.5 x 40.6)
Signed: R L Newman, lower right
Mrs. Walter Sharp, Brentwood, Tennessee

Provenance: Leon Deutsch, to E. C. Babcock, New York (1939), to the present owner, 1954.

References: Knoedler 1939, no. 32, under title *The Gypsy*; Virginia 1942, no. 7, under title *The Gypsy*; Tennessee Fine Arts Center, Nashville, *Tennessee Painting: The Past*, exhibition, May 22–July 31, 1960, no. 36, under title *The Gypsy*.

157 WOODLAND COMPANIONS
oil on canvas, 14 x 18 (35.6 x 45.7)
Mrs. William Penn Cresson, Stockbridge, Massachusetts

Provenance: Daniel Chester French, New York, purchased from the artist and presented to his daughter, the present owner.

References: Virginia 1942, no. 32.

158 WOODLAND COMPANIONS *figure 24*
oil on canvas, 14 x 18 (35.6 x 45.8)
Signed: R L Newman, lower right
Babcock Galleries, New York

Provenance: Nestor Sanborn, Brooklyn, New York, to E. C. Babcock, New York, 1926; Carmine Dalesio, New York (1954).

References: Whitney 1935, no. 16; Virginia 1942, no. 8, pl. 10.

159 WOODLAND SCENE
oil on canvas, $18\frac{5}{8}$ x $14\frac{5}{8}$ (47.3 x 37.2)
Victor D. Spark, New York, and Graham Gallery, New York

Provenance: Joseph Katz, Baltimore (1951).

References: Graham 1961, no. 24.

160 THE WOODLAND SPRING
oil on canvas, 14¼ x 24¾ (36.2 x 62.9)
Signed: R L Newman, lower right
Present location unknown

Provenance: Sir William C. Van Horne, Montreal (1894), purchased from the artist and passed on to his daughter Miss Adaline Van Horne (1934).

References: Knoedler 1894, no. 84; Boston 1894, no. 67.

161 WOOD NYMPH
oil on canvas, 5½ x 11½ (14 x 29.2)
Victor D. Spark, New York, and Graham Gallery, New York

Provenance: Henry J. Hardenburgh, New York (1894); New York art market, to Joseph Katz, Baltimore (1954).

References: Knoedler 1894, no. 101; Boston, 1894, no. 79; Graham 1961, no. 2, under title *Nymph in a Wood.*

Related Works: Girl Bathing, cat. no. 172.

162 YOUNG GIRL AND LOVE
oil on canvas, 18 x 24 (45.7 x 61)
Signed: R L Newman, at right
Present location unknown

Seated on a bank in a dark woodland, a young girl toys with Cupid at her knee. A glint of light is in the distant sky, and the red and white robe of the woman is brilliantly illuminated.

Provenance: Thomas B. Clarke, New York (1894), probably purchased from the artist; Clarke sale, American Art Association, New York, 1st evening sale, February 14, 1899, no. 18, under title *Woman and Love.*

References: Knoedler 1894, no. 16; Boston 1894, no. 12.

Drawings

163 HEAD OF A MAN
pencil, 9¾ x 8¾ (24.8 x 22.2)
The Montreal Museum of Fine Arts. Bequest of Miss Adaline Van Horne, 1945

Probably a self-portrait.

Provenance: Sir William C. Van Horne, Montreal, purchased from the artist and passed on to his daughter Miss Adaline Van Horne (1934).

164 SELF-PORTRAIT 1897
pencil, 9 x 6 (22.9 x 15.3)
Signed: R L Newman, December 4, 1897, lower left
Graham Gallery, New York

Provenance: Daniel Chester French, New York, gift of the artist; Mrs. Stewart Woodward, Chestnut Hill, Massachusetts, to the present owner.

165 ANTIOPE AND CUPID SLEEPING, after Correggio
chalk, 6¾ x 5 (17.2 x 12.7)
The Montreal Museum of Fine Arts. Bequest of Miss Adaline Van Horne, 1945

Inscribed: To W. C. Van Horne Esqr from R L N

Provenance: Gift of the artist to Sir William C. Van Horne, Montreal, passed on to his daughter Miss Adaline Van Horne (1934).

166 THE BATHER
charcoal, 7 x 5 (17.7 x 12.7)
Mr. Ira Glackens, Washington, D.C.

Inscribed: Drawing by Newman

Provenance: William J. Glackens, New York, probably purchased from the artist and passed on to his son, the present owner.

Related Works: *The Bather,* cat. no. 48.

167a BABY BOY LEARNING TO WALK (recto)
crayon, 8 1/16 x 3 3/4 (20.5 x 9.5)
Signed: R L Newman, lower center

167b GROUP OF CHILDREN (verso)
Mrs. William Penn Cresson, Stockbridge, Massachusetts

Provenance: Daniel Chester French, purchased from the artist and passed on to his daughter, the present owner.

168 EVENSONG *figure 21*
charcoal, 3 3/4 x 6 1/2 (9.5 x 14.5)
Signed: R L Newman, on mount
Private collection, Washington, D.C.

Provenance: Mrs. Andrew O'Connor, Jr.; Mrs. Frank H. Holden, New York (1935).

References: Virginia 1942, no. 41.

169 THE FATHER'S BLESSING
charcoal, 13 x 16 (33 x 41)
Present location unknown

Provenance: Sir William C. Van Horne, Montreal, purchase or gift from the artist; passed on to his daughter Miss Adaline Van Horne (1934).

170 FLOWERS
charcoal and pastel, 8 x 9¾ (20.3 x 24.8)
Graham Gallery, New York

Provenance: Daniel Chester French, New York, gift of the artist; Mrs. Stewart Woodward, Chestnut Hill, Massachusetts, to the present owner.

171 THE FORTUNE TELLER
crayon, 4 x 5⅛ (10.2 x 13)
Mr. and Mrs. Ferdinand H. Davis, New York

Provenance: William McKillop, New York (1935), passed on to Mrs. McKillop (1942); Plaza Art Galleries, New York, to present owner, 1973.

References: Whitney 1935, no. 34; Virginia 1942, no. 44; under title *Campfire Scene.*

Related Works: The Fortune Teller, fig. 56, cat. nos. 66-68; *The Sibyl,* cat. no. 142.

172 GIRL BATHING
pencil, 4¾ x 7 (12 x 17.8)
The Montreal Museum of Fine Arts. Bequest of Miss Adaline Van Horne, 1945

Provenance: Sir William C. Van Horne, Montreal, purchase or gift from the artist; passed on to his daughter Miss Adaline Van Horne (1934).

Related Works: Wood Nymph, cat. no. 161.

173 GRAPES
pencil, 7½ x 10¼ (19 x 26)
Graham Gallery, New York

Provenance: Daniel Chester French, New York, gift of the artist; Mrs. Stewart Woodward, Chestnut Hill, Massachusetts, to the present owner.

174 GRAPES
pencil, 7¾ x 10 (19.7 x 25.4)
Graham Gallery, New York

Provenance: Daniel Chester French, New York, gift of the artist; Mrs. Stewart Woodward, Chestnut Hill, Massachusetts, to the present owner.

175 HEAD OF A GIRL
charcoal, 9 x 8⅞ (22.9 x 22.5)
Mr. Ira Glackens, Washington, D.C.

Inscribed: Drawing by Newman

Provenance: William J. Glackens, New York, probably purchased from the artist and passed on to his son, the present owner.

176 HEAD OF A WOMAN
pencil, 12 x 9 (30.5 x 22.9)
University of Nebraska, Lincoln. Gift of the Milch Galleries, New York

Inscribed: R. L. Newman/To my friend Victor Harris/ 1895

Provenance: Victor Harris, New York, 1895; Milch Galleries, New York.

177 HEAD OF A YOUNG GIRL
pencil, 6½ x 6¾ (16.5 x 17.2)
The Montreal Museum of Fine Arts. Bequest of Miss Adaline Van Horne, 1945

Provenance: Sir William C. Van Horne, Montreal, gift or purchase from the artist, passed on to his daughter Miss Adaline Van Horne (1934).

178 HORSES IN A FIELD
pencil, 4 x 6½ (10.2 x 16.5)
Graham Gallery, New York

Provenance: Daniel Chester French, New York, gift of the artist; Mrs. Stewart Woodward, Chestnut Hill, Massachusetts, to the present owner.

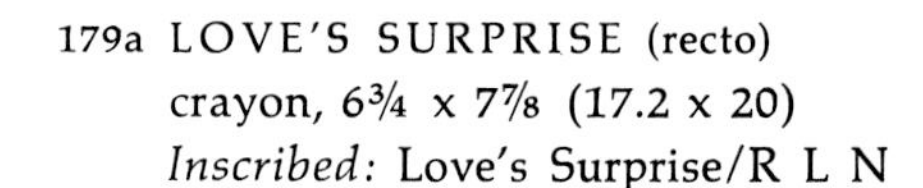

179a LOVE'S SURPRISE (recto)
crayon, $6\frac{3}{4}$ x $7\frac{7}{8}$ (17.2 x 20)
Inscribed: Love's Surprise/R L N

179b LANDSCAPE (verso)
pencil
Mrs. William Penn Cresson, Stockbridge, Massachusetts

Provenance: Daniel Chester French, New York, purchase or gift from the artist, passed on to his daughter, the present owner.

180 MADONNA AND CHILD
chalk, 10 x $7\frac{1}{2}$ (25.4 x 19)
The Montreal Museum of Fine Arts. Bequest of Miss Adaline Van Horne, 1945

Provenance: Sir William C. Van Horne, Montreal, probably purchased from the artist and passed on to his daughter, Miss Adaline Van Horne (1934).

Related Works: The Holy Family, fig. 18, cat. no. 25; *Girl and Two Children,* fig. 58, cat. no. 73.

181 THE MIRACULOUS DRAUGHT OF FISHES *figure 63*
pencil, $7\frac{15}{16}$ x $9\frac{15}{16}$ (20.2 x 25.2)
The Brooklyn Museum, Brooklyn, New York. Gift of Mr. William H. Fox (28.282)

References: Whitney 1935, no. 33; Virginia 1942, no. 38.

182 MOTHER AND CHILD IN LANDSCAPE *figure 65*
pencil, $6\frac{5}{8}$ x $10\frac{5}{8}$ (16.8 x 27)
Mrs. William Penn Cresson, Stockbridge, Massachusetts

Provenance: Daniel Chester French, New York, gift of the artist; passed on to his daughter, the present owner.

Related Works: Mother and Child, fig. 64, cat. no. 110.

183 NUDE
pencil, $3\frac{3}{4}$ x $3\frac{1}{8}$ (9.5 x 8)
Present location unknown

Provenance: Frederic Fairchild Sherman, Westport, Connecticut (1935); Macbeth Gallery, New York (1942).

References: Whitney 1935, no. 35; Virginia 1942, no. 42.

184 NUDE FIGURE OF A GIRL 1895
pencil, $11\frac{1}{2}$ x $9\frac{3}{8}$ (29.2 x 23.8)
Babcock Galleries, New York

Inscription: R. L. Newman/to his friend Victor Harris/ 1895

Provenance: Victor Harris, New York, 1895; Carmine Dalesio, New York, gift of Albert Milch.

185 RECLINING FIGURE
pencil, $6\frac{3}{4}$ x 8 (17.2 x 20.3)
The Montreal Museum of Fine Arts. Bequest of Miss Adaline Van Horne, 1945

Provenance: Sir William C. Van Horne, Montreal, purchased from the artist; passed on to his daughter Miss Adaline Van Horne (1934).

186a SAPPHO (recto)
pencil, $4\frac{3}{4}$ x $4\frac{1}{2}$ (12 x 11.5)
Signed: R L Newman, lower right

186b STUDY OF FEET (verso)
pencil, $9\frac{1}{2}$ x $7\frac{1}{4}$ (24.1 x 18.4)
Mrs. William Penn Cresson, Stockbridge, Massachusetts

Provenance: Daniel Chester French, New York, gift or purchase from the artist; passed on to his daughter, the present owner.

Related Works: *Sappho,* fig. 51, cat. no. 136.

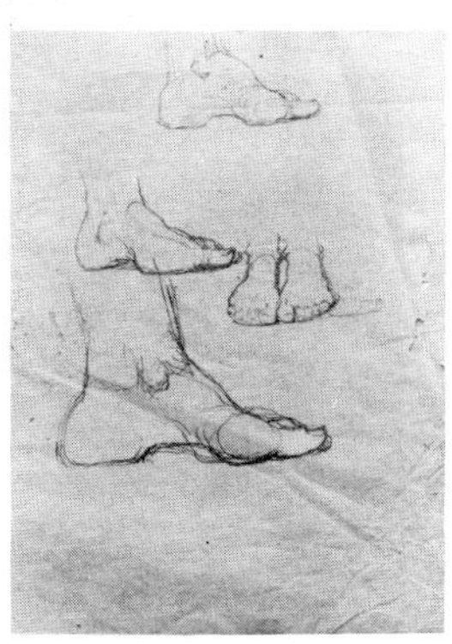

187 SHEEP, after Millet
pencil, $8\frac{1}{4}$ x $9\frac{1}{2}$ (21 x 24)
The Montreal Museum of Fine Arts. Bequest of Miss Adaline Van Horne, 1945

Provenance: Sir William C. Van Horne, Montreal, gift or purchase from the artist; passed on to his daughter Miss Adaline Van Horne (1934).

Related Works: Sheep, fig. 26, cat. no. 138.

188 SKETCH OF MRS. HOLDEN AS A GIRL
pencil, 10 x 8 (25.4 x 20.3)
Present location unknown

Provenance: Mrs. Frank H. Holden, New York (1935).

References: Whitney 1935, no. 32; Virginia, 1942, no. 43.

189 STUDY FOR THE MARYS AT THE TOMB: 3 FIGURES *figure 39*
charcoal, 3 x $2\frac{3}{4}$ (7.6 x 7)
The Brooklyn Museum, Brooklyn, New York (31.205A)

References: Whitney 1935, no. 36; Virginia 1942, no. 39.

190 STUDY FOR THE THREE MARYS AT THE TOMB: FOUR FIGURES *figure 40*
charcoal, 3 x $2\frac{7}{8}$ (7.6 x 7.3)
The Brooklyn Museum, Brooklyn, New York (31.205B)

References: Whitney 1935, no. 36; Virginia 1942, no. 40.

191 STUDY OF A NUDE FIGURE
pencil, $6\frac{3}{4}$ x $7\frac{3}{4}$ (17.2 x 19.7)
The Montreal Museum of Fine Arts. Bequest of Miss Adaline Van Horne, 1945

Provenance: Sir William C. Van Horne, Montreal, purchased from the artist and passed on to his daughter Miss Adaline Van Horne (1934).

192 TREES *figure 22*
pencil, 4 x 5½ (10.2 x 14)
Graham Gallery, New York

Provenance: Daniel Chester French, New York, gift of the artist; Mrs. Stewart Woodward, Chestnut Hill, Massachusetts, to the present owner.

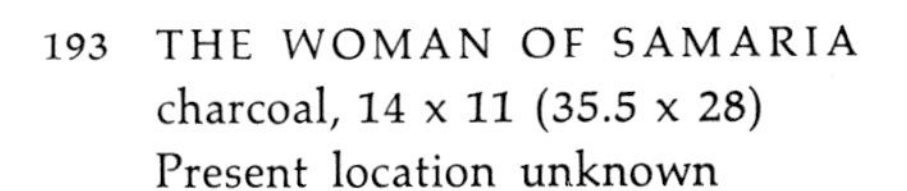

193 THE WOMAN OF SAMARIA
charcoal, 14 x 11 (35.5 x 28)
Present location unknown

Provenance: Sir William C. Van Horne, Montreal, purchased from the artist; passed on to his daughter Miss Adaline Van Horne (1934).

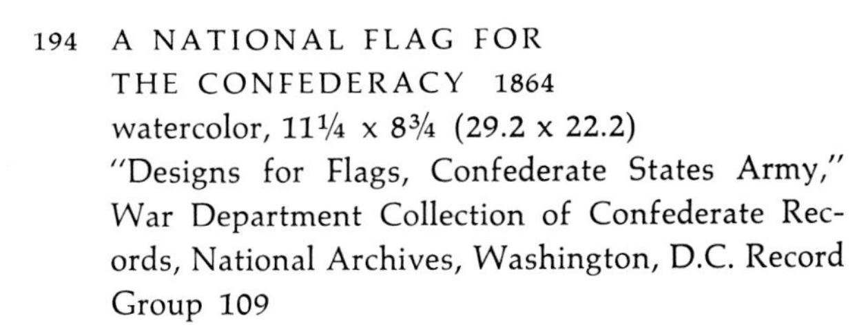

194 A NATIONAL FLAG FOR THE CONFEDERACY 1864
watercolor, 11¼ x 8¾ (29.2 x 22.2)
"Designs for Flags, Confederate States Army," War Department Collection of Confederate Records, National Archives, Washington, D.C. Record Group 109

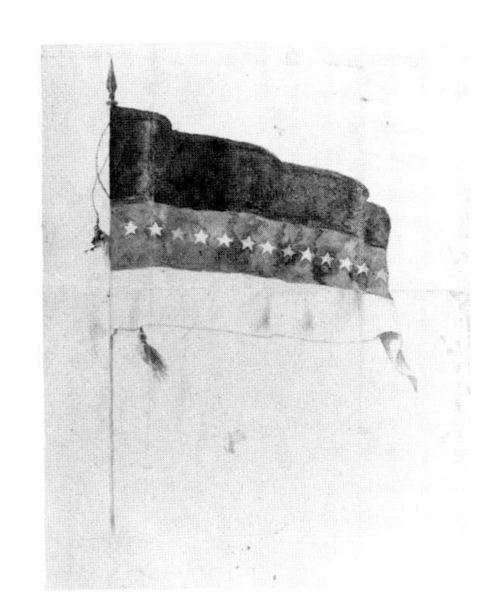

Newman submitted this design, with an accompanying letter, to Jefferson Davis on March 12, 1864. The red field at the top and the white field at the bottom are separated by a blue band with fourteen, five-pointed, white stars, only thirteen of which are shown. Each star represents a state of the Confederacy, and the fact that there are fourteen indicates the anticipation that Maryland, Kentucky, and Missouri would secede from the Union.

Bibliography

Entries are arranged chronologically within each category, except for Sources and Books, which are arranged alphabetically.

SOURCES

Boston (Massachusetts) Public Library. Manuscript Section. Newman to Bartlett, October 1, 1881.

Brooklyn Museum Quarterly (New York) 8 (October 1921). Contains Nestor Sanborn's notes on Newman's life, "Robert Loftin Newman, Colorist," pp. 157–61.

The Frick Art Reference Library (New York). Daniel Chester French to Frederic Fairchild Sherman, April 25, 1919.

———. Nestor Sanborn to Frederic Fairchild Sherman, April 17, 1919.

Marchal E. Landgren Papers. In private possession. Washington, D.C.

Montgomery County Records (Clarksville, Tennessee):

Register's Office. Deed Books Nos. 4–8, 14, 19, 52 include records of various transactions involving properties of Newman.

Clerk's Office. Book J. "Joseph Winston's Will"; Marriage Record Book 3, "John L. Swaney [sic] to Mrs. S. J. Winston, August 27, 1860."

Chancery Court Clerk and Master's Office. Minutes Book 25, "R. Lemmons, et al, vs. J. B. Shearer." Gives date of Newman's mother's death as 1873.

Nashville (Tennessee) *Union and Republican,* December 12, 1872. Contains Robert Loftin Newman's only known printed work: "Museums of Art: Musée du Louvre." Copy on file in Marchal E. Landgren Papers.

National Archives, Washington, D.C. Record Group 109. "Rebel Archives, War Department, Record Division." Contains Newman's service record with the Confederate army.

The New York Public Library. Manuscript Division. Asher B. Durand Papers. Newman to Durand, December 22, 1846.

Tennessee State Library and Archives (Nashville). Manuscript Section. William W. Fergusson Papers. Newman to Fergusson, December 7, 1872.

Virginia Marriage Bonds, Richmond City. Reddy, Anne Waller, and Andrew Lewis Riffe, comps. Vol. 1. Staunton, Virginia, 1939. Contains dates of marriages of Newman's mother to Robert Newman and to Joseph Winston.

Walter Sharp Papers. Incorporated in Marchal E. Landgren Papers.

BOOKS

Barker, Virgil. *American Painting: History and Interpretation.* New York: Macmillan, 1950.

Baur, John I. H. *American Painting in the Nineteenth Century: Main Trends and Movements.* New York: Praeger, 1953.

———. *Revolution and Tradition in Modern American Art.* Cambridge: Harvard University Press, 1951.

Corcoran Gallery of Art, Washington, D.C. *Catalogue of the Collection of American Paintings.* Vol. 1, *Painters Born before 1850.* Washington, D.C., 1966.

Dictionary of American Biography. 11 vols. New York: Charles Scribner's Sons, 1943–1964, 7:465.

Gerdts, William H., and Russell Burke. *American Still-Life Painting.* New York: Praeger, 1971.

Green, Samuel M. *American Art: A Historical Survey.* New York: Ronald Press Company, 1966.

Hartmann, Sadakichi. *A History of American Art.* New rev. ed., 2 vols. Boston: L. C. Page, 1932.

La Follette, Suzanne. *Art in America.* New York: Harper & Brothers, 1929.

Larkin, Oliver W. *Art and Life in America.* Rev. and enl. ed. New York: Holt, Rinehart and Winston, 1960.

The Metropolitan Museum of Art (New York). *Catalogue of Paintings* by Bryson Burroughs. 9th ed. New York, 1931.

Mumford, Lewis. *The Brown Decades.* 2d rev. ed., New York: Dover Publications, 1955.

National Cyclopedia of American Biography. 53 vols. and 10 supps. to date. New York: J. T. White & Company, 1893–, 13: 179.

The Phillips Collection (Washington, D.C.). *The Phillips Collection, a Museum of Modern Art and its Sources. Catalogue.* Washington, D.C., 1952.

Phillips, Duncan. *A Collection in the Making.* New York: E. Weyhe, 1960; and Washington: Phillips Memorial Gallery, 1926.

Pierson, William H., and Martha Davidson, eds. *Arts of the United States; a Pictorial Survey.* New York: McGraw-Hill, 1960.

Sherman, Frederic Fairchild. *Landscape and Figure Painters of America.* New York, 1917. Includes his "Robert Loftin Newman, an American Colorist," first published in *Art in America* 4 (April 1916). Privately printed.

Soby, James Thrall, and Dorothy C. Miller. *Romantic Painting in America.* New York: Museum of Modern Art, 1943. Includes catalog of the exhibition of the same title held at the Museum of Modern Art (New York), November 1943–February 6, 1944.

EXHIBITION CATALOGS

Knoedler (M.) & Company (New York). *Loan Collection of Paintings by Mr. R. L. Newman*; exhibition, March 1–15, 1894, New York, 1894. Folder.

Museum of Fine Arts (Boston). *R. L. Newman*; exhibition, March 27–April 17, 1894. Boston, 1894. Folder.

The Brooklyn Museum (New York). *Works of American Painters 1860–1885*; a Special Historical Exhibition to Celebrate the Opening of the Catskill Aqueduct, November 1–29, 1917. Brooklyn, 1917.

Frank K. M. Rehn Galleries (New York). *Loan Collection of Paintings by Robert Loftin Newman*; exhibition, April 14–May 5, 1924. New York, 1924. Folder.

Whitney Museum of American Art (New York). *Paintings by Robert Loftin Newman*; exhibition, January 15–February 8, 1935. Introd. by Marchal E. Landgren. New York, 1935.

Knoedler (M.) & Company (New York). *Two American Romantics of the Nineteenth Century, Robert Loftin Newman and Albert Pinkham Ryder*; exhibition, November 13–December 2, 1939. Introd. by Marchal E. Landgren. New York, 1939. Folder.

Carnegie Institute (Pittsburgh). Department of Fine Arts. *Survey of American Painting*; exhibition, October 24–December 15, 1940. Pittsburgh, 1940.

Virginia Museum of Fine Arts (Richmond). *A Memorial Exhibition of the Work of Robert Loftin Newman*, January 26–February 27, 1942. With an introductory critique and biography by Marchal E. Landgren. Richmond, 1942.

Newark Museum (Newark, New Jersey). *A Museum in Action.* Catalog of an exhibition of American paintings and sculpture from the museum's collections, with an introduction by Holger Cahill, October 31, 1944–January 31, 1945. Newark, 1944.

Hundert Jahre americkanische Maleri 1800–1900; exhibition, Städelsches Kunstinstitut, Frankfurt, Germany, March 14–May 3, 1953, et al. Texts by John I. H. Baur, H. K. Röthel, and A. Schädler. Munich, 1953.

Tennessee Fine Arts Center (Nashville). *Tennessee Painting: the Past*; exhibition, May 22–July 31, 1960. Nashville, 1960.

Graham Gallery (New York). *Robert Loftin Newman*; exhibition, September 20–October 21, 1961. New York, 1961. Folder, with insert.

University of Maryland Art Gallery (College Park). *American Pupils of Thomas Couture*; exhibition, March 19–April 26, 1970. Text and catalog by Marchal E. Landgren. College Park, 1970.

The Hand and the Spirit: Religious Art in America 1700–1900; exhibition sponsored by the Graduate Theological Seminary, Berkeley; the University Art Museum, Berkeley; and the National Collection of Fine Arts, Washington, D.C., 1972–1973. Texts by Joshua C. Taylor and Jane Dillenberger. Berkeley, 1972.

PERIODICALS

"The Newman Exhibition at Knoedler's." *The Critic*, no. 629, March 10, 1894.

Sherman, Frederic Fairchild. "Robert Loftin Newman, an American Colorist." *Art in America* 4 (April 1916): 177–84.

"Mother and Child." *Bridgeport* (Connecticut) *Life*, January 12, 1935.

"Newman's Art Shown at Whitney." *Art News*, January 19, 1935, p. 6.

Mumford, Lewis. "The Art Galleries." *New Yorker*, January 26, 1935.

Landgren, Marchal E. "Robert Loftin Newman." *American Magazine of Art* 28 (March 1935): 134–40.

Code, Grant. "American Painting in the Collection of the Brooklyn Museum." *Brooklyn Museum Quarterly* 24 (April 1937): 47–78.

Sherman, Frederic Fairchild. "Robert Loftin Newman." *Art in America* 27 (April 1939): 73–75.

Lane, James W. "A View of Two Native Romantics." *Art News*, November 11, 1939, p. 9.

"Ryder and Newman, Kindred Spirits." *Art Digest*, November 15, 1939, p. 13.

Coates, Robert M. "The Art Galleries." *New Yorker*, November 25, 1939.

Breuning, Margaret. "Ryder and Newman." *Magazine of Art* 32 (December 1939): 714–16.

"Memorial Exhibition for Two Virginia Artists." *Virginia Museum of Fine Arts Bulletin* 2 (January 1, 1942): unpaged.

"Virginia Honors Two Native Sons." *Art Digest*, February 15, 1942, p. 12.

"Virginia Honors Myers and Newman." *Art News*, February 1–14, 1942, p. 8.

"A Poetic Colorist." *Pictures on Exhibit* 5 (February 1942): 14–15.

"Additions Made to the Permanent Collection of the Addison Gallery between July 1942 and July 1943." *Addison Gallery of American Art Bulletin*, 1943.

Caldwell, Henry B. "A Romantic Painting by Newman." *Corcoran Gallery of Art Bulletin* 3 (January 1951): 13–16.

Review of exhibition at Graham Gallery. *Arts* 36 (November 1961): 46.

Review of exhibition at Graham Gallery. *Art News* 60 (November 1961): 16–17.

Smith, David Loeffler. "Romanticism and the American Tradition." *American Artist* 26 (March 1962): 28.

Boime, Albert. "Newman, Ryder, Couture, and Hero-Worship in Art History." *American Art Journal* 3 (Fall 1971): 5–22.

Brumbaugh, Thomas B. "Letters of Robert Loftin Newman, a Tennessee Artist." *Tennessee Historical Quarterly* 32 (Summer 1973): 107–23.

NEWSPAPERS

Review of the exhibition at Knoedler's. *New York Tribune*, March 4, 1894.

Review of the exhibition at Knoedler's. *New York Post*, March 3, 1894.

"The Newman Exhibit." *Boston Daily Advertiser*, March 30, 1894.

"The Fine Arts: The Newman Exhibition and the Whistler Paintings at the Museum of Fine Arts." *Boston Sunday Herald*, April 1, 1894.

Obituary. *New York American*, April 1, 1912.

Obituary. *New York Call*, April 1, 1912.

Obituary. *New York Herald*, April 1, 1912.

Obituary. *New York Sun*, April 1, 1912.

Obituary. *New York Times*, April 1, 1912.

Obituary. *New York Tribune*, April 1, 1912.

Obituary. *New York World*, April 1, 1912.

Obituary. *Clarksville* (Tennessee) *Leaf-Chronicle*, April 24, 1912.

Jewell, Edward Alden. "Whitney Museum Opens 3 Exhibits: Newman Paintings Hung." *New York Times*, January 16, 1935.

Vaughan, Malcolm. "In the Art Galleries . . . Forgotten American Master." *New York American*, January 19, 1935.

Breuning, Margaret. "Whitney Museum Shows Recent Acquisitions." *New York Post*, January 19, 1935.

"Attractions in the Galleries." *New York Sun*, January 19, 1935.

"Museum's Purchases Defended." *New York World-Telegram*, January 19, 1935.

Cortissoz, Royal. "A Revival of Fortuny and his School." *New York Herald-Tribune*, January 20, 1935.

Jewell, Edward Alden. "The Whitney Presents—." *New York Times*, January 20, 1935.

[McCausland, Elizabeth.] "Adventures in Discovery of an American Painter." *Springfield* (Massachusetts) *Sunday Union and Republican*, January 20, 1935.

Klein, Jerome. "Art Comment: Two Romantics." *New York Post*, November 18, 1939.

McBride, Henry M. "Ryder and Newman." *New York Sun*, November 18, 1939.

Genauer, Emily. "Joint Show of Ryder, Newman." *New York World-Telegram*, November 18, 1939.

"American Art: Robert L. Newman, Albert P. Ryder and Some Artists of the Present Day." *New York Herald-Tribune*, November 19, 1939.

Breuning, Margaret. "In the World of Art." *New York Journal and American*, November 19, 1939.

"Ryder and Newman." *New York Times*, November 19, 1939.

"Newman and Ryder Linked as American Romantics." *Springfield* (Massachusetts) *Union and Republican*, December 3, 1939.

"Museum Here Seeks Works of Newman." *Richmond* (Virginia) *Times-Dispatch*, January 4, 1942.

"Memorial Exhibit to Include Works by Virginia-Born Artists." *Richmond* (Virginia) *Times-Dispatch*, January 11, 1942.

"Art Exhibits Will Mark Anniversary." *Richmond* (Virginia) *Times-Dispatch*, January 15, 1942.

"Robert L. Newman Paintings to be Exhibited in City." *Richmond* (Virginia) *Times-Dispatch*, January 16, 1942.

"State Museum will Observe Anniversary." *Richmond* (Virginia) *Times-Dispatch*, January 19, 1942.

"Two Virginians' Paintings go on Exhibit." *Richmond* (Virginia) *Times-Dispatch*, January 26, 1942.

Vautibault, Elizabeth de. "Seeing is Believing: The Myers-Newman Memorial Show at the Virginia Museum." *Richmond* (Virginia) *News Leader*, January 30, 1942.

Staff of the Exhibition

Guest director for this exhibition was Marchal E. Landgren. David Keeler directed the presentation of the exhibition aided by Frank Caldwell, technical assistant. Val Lewton designed the installation which was supervised by John Fleming. Exhibition preparators were Gervis Perkins, Robert Bernstein, and James Maynor. Ralph Logan prepared the graphics, George Navin constructed the installation, and Oliver Anderson prepared frames for hanging. William Walker and other members of the NPG-NCFA Library staff offered research assistance, and H. Nichols B. Clark aided Mr. Landgren with details in research. Benjamin P. Ruhe supervised publicity, assisted by Alison Fujino. Robert Johnston, registrar, and Burgess Coleman, assistant registrar, arranged loans for the exhibition. They were assisted by Lenore Sams and Deborah Jensen. Robert L. Dean handled details concerning building preparations. Editor for the catalog was Carroll S. Clark, assisted by Polly Roulhac. Lowell Anson Kenyon assisted with the photography; he was aided by Heather Noble.

The following photographs are through the courtesy of The Brooklyn Museum, figure 5; Archives Photographiques, figure 7; Victoria & Albert Museum, figure 27; and The Metropolitan Museum of Art, figure 42.

RECENT PUBLICATIONS AVAILABLE FROM THE NATIONAL COLLECTION OF FINE ARTS

George Caleb Bingham 1811–1879. Introduction by David W. Scott. Essay by E. Maurice Bloch. 99 pages; 36 b&w illustrations. 1967. $.75.

Charles Sheeler. Foreword by David W. Scott. Introduction by Harry Lowe. Biographical notes by Abigail Booth. Essays by Martin Friedman, Charles Millard, and Bartlett Hayes. Three essays by Charles Sheeler. 156 pages; 158 b&w illustrations; 4 color plates. 1968. $5.95.

Milton Avery. Introduction by Adelyn D. Breeskin. Commemorative essay by Mark Rothko. 96 pages; 129 b&w illustrations; 10 color plates. 1969. $4.98.

Leonard Baskin. Foreword by Joshua C. Taylor. Essay by Alan Fern with annotations by Leonard Baskin. 76 pages; 62 b&w illustrations. 1970. $1.50.

H. Lyman Saÿen. Foreword by Joshua C. Taylor. Essay by Adelyn D. Breeskin. 84 pages; 50 b&w illustrations; 2 color plates. 1970. $2.50.

Jasper F. Cropsey: 1823–1900. Foreword by Joshua C. Taylor. Essay by William S. Talbot. 114 pages; 92 b&w illustrations; 4 color plates. 1970. $2.50.

Romaine Brooks, "Thief of Souls." Introduction by Joshua C. Taylor. Essay by Adelyn D. Breeskin. 143 pages; 18 b&w illustrations; 2 color plates. 1971. $3.50.

William H. Johnson. Introduction by Joshua C. Taylor. Essay by Adelyn D. Breeskin. 208 pages; 168 b&w illustrations; 1 color plate. 1971. $4.25.

Drawings by William Glackens. Foreword by Joshua C. Taylor. Background by Ira Glackens. Essay by Janet A. Flint. 23 pages; 12 b&w illustrations. 1972. $1.00.

Two American Painters: Fritz Scholder and T. C. Cannon. Foreword by Joshua C. Taylor. Essay by Robert A. Ewing. 45 pages; 13 b&w illustrations; 2 color plates. 1972. $1.25.

National Parks and the American Landscape. Foreword by Joshua C. Taylor. Essay by William H. Truettner and Robin Bolton-Smith. 141 pages; 117 b&w illustrations; 3 color plates. 1972. $3.25.

Alfred H. Maurer. Foreword by Joshua C. Taylor. Essay by Sheldon Reich. 167 pages; 155 b&w illustrations; 3 color plates. 1973. $4.75.

Lilly Martin Spencer (1822–1902): The Joys of Sentiment. Introduction by Joshua C. Taylor. Essay by Robin Bolton-Smith and William H. Truettner. Annotated list of known works. 256 pages; 133 b&w illustrations; 5 color plates. 1973. $6.25.

Marguerite Zorach: The Early Years, 1908-1920. Foreword by Joshua C. Taylor. Essay by Roberta K. Tarbell. 77 pages; 43 b&w illustrations; 3 color plates. 1973. $2.90.

Art of the Pacific Northwest: From the 1930s to the Present. Introduction by Joshua C. Taylor. Essays by Rachael Griffin and Martha Kingsbury. 142 pages; 143 b&w illustrations; 5 color plates. 1974. $4.10.

These publications can be ordered from the Museum Shop, National Collection of Fine Arts, Smithsonian Institution, Washington, D.C. 20560